Also by Thelma Kandel
WHAT WOMEN EARN   (Linden/S&S 1981)

Thelma Kandel

What to Name the Cat

Illustrated by Mimi Vang Olsen

Linden Press/ S & S
NEW YORK 1983

To Mike, Bethany and Andrew.
And Truffles.

Copyright © 1983 by Thelma Kandel

All rights reserved
including the right of reproduction
in whole or in part in any form
Published by Linden Press/Simon & Schuster
A Division of Simon & Schuster, Inc.
Simon & Schuster Building
Rockefeller Center
1230 Avenue of the Americas
New York, New York 10020

LINDEN PRESS/SIMON & SCHUSTER and colophon are trademarks of
Simon & Schuster, Inc.

Designed by Karolina Harris
Manufactured in the United States of America

10 9 8 7 6 5 4 3 2 1

Library of Congress Cataloging in Publication Data
Kandel, Thelma, date.
    What to name the cat.

    1. Cats—Names.   I. Title.
SF442.4.K36   1983   636.8   83-9342
ISBN 0-671-46000-5
    0-671-47307-7 Pbk.

Contents

Introduction

There are more than thirty-four million cats in America, and sooner or later they all need names. Between these covers are thousands of cat names you've probably never heard or thought of. From common alley cats to rare, expensive breeds; short hair, long hair or wire hair —they all deserve the best in feline monikers.

Look in the Biblical section for divine inspiration, or under Astronomy if your pet is a heavenly body. There are names for finicky felines; names for felines *fatales*; names of celebrated cats and celebrities' cats; names for pets of doctors, lawyers and Indian chiefs; architects; writers and poets; computer whizzes; engineers and mathematicians; dancers; musicians; theater and television buffs; fashion followers; sports enthusiasts; gourmets—and more.

The U.S. Census defines a human cohabiter as a POSSLQ, Person of the Opposite Sex Sharing Living Quarters; but "Posslq" (pronounced possilcue) would be a dandy name for a cat when translated as Pet of Optimum Satisfaction Sharing Living Quarters. A cat that is an unexpected acquisition might be named "Foundit," "Freebie" or "Gratis." How about "Lagniappe" (pronounced lan-yap), meaning bonus or prize? or "Beshert" (Yiddish, fated)? or try "Serendipity" for the kitty that's a happy surprise.

Why settle for the mundane when you can give your pet a name that's the cat's meow? Herein lies a smorgasbord of old standbys, classical and charismatic names and so much more; names for a clowder of cats and a kindle of kittens. So browse and search herein— the purrfect name is waiting for you.

T.K.

What to Name the Cat

Appetites

Food

Food	**Drink**
Albertus Magnus (13th-century food writer)	Abboccato
Amanita (mushroom genus)	Absinthe
Ambrosia	Almadén
Amphitryon (legendary Greek lavish host)	Amara
	Amaretto
	Amontillado
	Amstel
	Angostura
	Anisette
	Apollinaris
	Applejack
	Armagnac
	Asti Spumante
Baba au Rhum	Bacardi
Biscuit	Barbella
Bistro	Barbera
Bonbon	Bardolino
Bouillon	Beaujolais

Brandy Alexander
Bumbo (British cold punch)

Cadbury
Camembert
Canapé
Chanterelle (mushroom)
Charlotte Russe
Chateaubriand
Chicory
Chipwich
Chutney
Craig Claiborne
Cranberry
Creamsicle
Crouton
Cruller
Crumpet

Cabernet
Campari
Cassis
Chablis
Chambertin
Chardonnay
Chartreuse
Chianti
Chivas Regal
Chugalug
Cider
Cinzano
Claret
Cognac
Cointreau
Coonawara
Coors
Courvoisier

Dabberlocks (edible seaweed)
De Gustibus (Lat., a matter of taste)

Daiquiri
Dewars

Dumpling

Eclair
Endive
Epicurus (Roman taste-setter)
Escoffier (French food expert)

Fetticus (corn salad)
Filbert
Fondue
Fritter
Fudgsicle

Gherkin
Gorgonzola
Granola
Griddlecake

Dinkelacker
Dom Perignon
Drambuie
Dubonnet

Fernet Branca
Fino
Folonari
Frangelico
Frascati

Galliano
Gattinara
Gibson
Gilbeys
Glenfiddich
Glenlivet
Glogg
Grand Marnier

Hominy
Hot Fudge

Kabob
Kamchatka (caviar)
Kefir
Kikkoman
Kohlrabi

Larousse (gastronomic dictionary)
Liederkranz
Limburger
Linguine
Lucullus (Roman epicure)

Grenadine
Guinness Stout

Harvey Wallbanger
Haut Brion
Heineken
Horchata

Jack Daniel's
Jim Beam
John Barleycorn

Korbel
Kronenbourg

Lafite
Lambrusco
Lillet

Macadamia
Macaroon
Madeleine
Malagkit (Philippine rice)
Mangel-Wurzel (beet)
Mango
Maraschino
Melanthus (ancient Greek epicure)
Meringue
Molasses
Mozzarella
Muffin
Mulberry
Mulligatawny

Nougat

Okra
Osestrova (caviar)

Parmentier

Madeira
Manzanilla
Margarita
Marsala
Martini
Mateus
Midori
Mint Julep
Mirassou
Montrachet
Morat
Mouton-Rothschild
Muscadet

Negroni
Neuchâtel

Orvieto
Orzata
Ouzo

Perrier

Pasta
Peperoni
Persimmon
Philoxenus (ancient Greek gourmet)
Pignolo
Pistachio
Pomegranate
Popover
Praline
Prosciutto
Pumpernickel

Quahog
Quiche

Ramekin
Rhubarb
Romaine
Roquefort
Rutabaga

Sacher Torte
Salami

Piper Heidsieck
Pommery
Pousse-Café
Punt e Mes

Raki
Refosco
Rémy Martin
Retsina
Rob Roy
Ruffino

Saint-Emilion
Sake

Salsify

Sassafras

Scampi

Semolina

Sherbet

Sorbet

Soufflé

Sprinkles

Spud

Stilton

Strudel

Succotash

Sukiyaki

Tabasco

Tamale

Tartare

Tetrazzini

Theobroma (Gr., food of the gods)

Tiffin (English light lunch)

Tofutti (Tofu ice cream)

Tortilla

Treacle

Truffles

Sambuca

Sangría

Sarsaparilla

Sauvignon

Sazerac

Schweppes

Smirnoff

Soave

Stolichnaya

Strega

Swizzle

Syllabub

Taittinger

Tanqueray

Tavel

Tequila

Tía Maria

Toddy

Tom Collins

Tuborg

Tullamore Dew

Tullibardine

Uneeda Biscuit

Usquebaugh (Gaelic, whiskey)

Valpolicella
Verdicchio
Vermouth
Vichy
Vodka
V.S.O.P. (Very Superior Old Pale)

Waffles
Worcestershire

Watneys
Whiskey

Yogurt

Ziti
Zucchini

Zinfandel

Foreign Foods

Allumette (Fr., matchstick potato)

Baba Ganoush (Middle East, chick-pea salad)
Baguette (Fr., small, long bread)
Baklava (Gr., pastry)
Béchamel (Fr., white sauce)
Blini (Rus., crêpes)
Bok Choy (Chinese cabbage)
Bon Vivant (Fr., epicure)
Bordelaise (Fr., brown sauce)
Brioche (French roll)

Cacciatore (Ital., hunter-style)
Café Noir (Fr., black coffee)
Cannella (Ital., cinnamon)
Cannelloni (Italian pastry)
Cassata (Ital., ice cream)
Champignon (Fr., mushroom)
Chevapchichi (Yugoslavian skewered meat)
Couscous (Moroccan stew)
Crêpe Suzette (Fr., thin pancake with brandy)

Croissant (Fr., crescent-shaped roll)

Daikon (Jap., radish)
Diable (Fr., deviled)

Enoki (Jap., mushroom)
Escargot (Fr., snail)

Falafel (Israeli vegetable fritter)
Fettuccine (Ital., noodles in cream sauce)
Flummery (English custard)
Fregalette (Ital., little strawberry)
Fritella (Ital., fritter)

Gâteau (Fr., cake)
Gazpacho (Span., cold spicy tomato soup)
Guacamole (Span., avocado dip)

Halvah (Arabic sesame-seed candy)
Hamantash (Jewish poppy-seed or prune holiday
  pastry)

Haricot (Fr., string bean)

Imbiss (Ger., snack)

Kalamata (Gr., olive)
Kipfel (Ger., small roll)
Klopse (Ger., meatball)
Knedlicky (Czech., dumpling)
Kugel (Jewish noodle pudding)

Manzanita (Span., little apple)
Marron (Fr., chestnut)
Marscapone (Italian cheese)
Matsutake (Japanese mushroom)
Miel (Fr., honey)
Mignonette (Fr., coarsely ground pepper)
Mirabelle (Fr., yellowish plum)
Morel (Fr., mushroom)
Mornay (Fr., sauce)
Moussaka (Greek meat-and-eggplant dish)
Mousse (French dessert)

Nameko (Japanese orange mushroom)
Nosher (Yiddish, nibbler)

Pamplemousse (Fr., grapefruit)
Panettone (Italian fruitcake)
Panino (Ital., sandwich roll)
Pirogi (Russ., meat-filled pastry)
Pistou (Fr., basil sauce)

Radicchio (Ital., red winter lettuce)
Ratatouille (Fr., eggplant and peppers)
Rémoulade (French sauce)
Risotto (Italian rice dish)

Sabayon (Fr., wine-and-egg sauce)
Sally Lunn (English teacake)
Shashlik (Middle Eastern barbecued lamb)
Shish Kabob (Middle Eastern skewered meat &
  vegetables)
Souvlaki (Gr., barbecued lamb)
Spätzle (Ger., dumpling)
Spumoni (Italian ice cream)

Tabouli (Middle Eastern bulgur wheat salad)
Tahini (Israeli sauce for falafel)
Tamar (Hebrew, date)
Tandoori (Indian herbed style of cooking)

Tarama (Gr., caviar spread)
Tartufo (Ital., truffle)
Tchorba (Yugos., chicken soup)
Tofu (Jap., soybean cake)
Torrone (Italian candy)
Tzimmes (Jewish carrots and honey)

Vichyssoise (Fr., cold potato soup)

Wasabi (Jap., horseradish)

Zabaglione (Ital., wine-and-egg sauce)
Zeppole (Italian doughnut)

Pairs:

Alka & Seltzer
Bagels & Lox
Bromo & Seltzer
Bourbon & Soda
Bubble & Squeak (English, beef & brussels
   sprouts)
Cece & Garbanzo (chick-peas)
Chitlings & Grits
Chow Mein & Lo Mein
Doch & Dorris
Gin & Tonic
Gin & Vermouth

Lichi & Kiwi
Martini & Rossi
Moët & Chandon
Pepsi & Coke
Ravioli & Tortelloni
Sevruga & Beluga (caviar)
Spumoni & Tortoni
Sushi & Sashimi (Japanese raw-fish dishes)
Tempura & Sukiyaki
Whiskey & Soda
Wonton & Dim Sum (Chinese dumplings)

Names for Wine Lovers:

Balthazar (16-quart bottle)
Demijohn (narrow-necked bottle holding up to 10 gallons)
Firkin (9-gallon cask)
Jeroboam (4-quart bottle)
Magnum (double bottle)
Methuselah (8-quart bottle)
Nebuchadnezzar (20-quart bottle)
Puncheon (84-gallon cask)
Rehoboam (6-quart bottle)

Rundlet (18-gallon cask)
Salmanazar (12-quart bottle)

Kottabos (ancient Greek game using the remnants in the wine cup to hit a saucer and win kisses from the other players)
Oenophilia (Lat., love of wine)
Propeno Tibi (Lat., I drink to you)
Temperance Fugit (Lat., pun meaning temperance flees)

Artists, Sculptors & Architects

Archipenko

Beardsley
Bellini
Benvenuto Cellini
Botero
Botticelli
Buckminster Fuller
Brancusi

Calder
Canaletto
Caravaggio
Cassatt
Cézanne
Chagall
Constable
Correggio

Dada
Dali

Daumier
De Chirico
De Kooning
Delacroix
Della Robbia
Dine
Donatello
Dubuffet

El Greco
Erté

Fra Filippo Lippi
Fragonard
Frankenthaler
Frank Lloyd Wright

Gainsborough
Gauguin
Giacometti
Gioconda (Ital., name for the *Mona Lisa*)

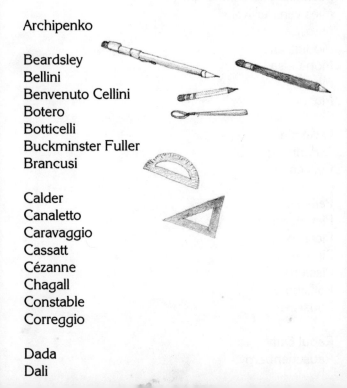

Giotto
Grandma Moses

Hieronymus Bosch
Hockney
Hundertwasser

I. M. Pei
Inigo Jones

Jackson Pollock
Jasper Johns

Kandinsky
Kokoschka

Léger
Leonardo da Vinci
Lichtenstein
Lysippus

Magritte
Maja (the reclining nude by Goya)
Manet

Marcel Duchamp
Matisse
Michelangelo Buonarroti
Mies van der Rohe
Miró
Modigliani
Mona Lisa
Monet
Mucha

O'Keeffe
Oldenburg
Orozco

Palladio
Piet Mondrian
Picasso
Piranesi
Pissarro
Pollaiuolo
Poussin

Raoul Dufy
Rauschenberg

Rembrandt van Rijn
Renoir
Rockwell
Rodin
Rosenquist
Rothko
Rouault
Rousseau
Rubens

Saarinen
Seurat
Starnina

Taliesin

Tchelitchew
Tiepolo
Tinguely
Tintoretto
Trova

Utrillo

Van Dyke
Van Gogh
Velásquez
Vermeer
Verrocchio

Watteau

Pairs:

Currier & Ives
Pablo & Picasso

Toulouse & Lautrec
Winslow & Homer

Astronomy & Astrology

Aldebaran (reddish-orange star in Taurus)
Alpha Centauri (3 stars that appear to be one because of their brightness)
Alpha Hercules (largest star in our galaxy)
Altair (white star)
Andromeda (constellation)
Antares (red star in Scorpius)
Aphelion (farthest point from the sun of a heavenly body's orbit)
Apogee (farthest point from the earth of planets around the sun)
Aquila (constellation, the Eagle)
Arcturus (orange star)
Arend-Roland (a comet)
Argo (constellation)
Ariel (satellite of Uranus)
Aristarchus (brightest moon crater)
Artemis (Greek moon goddess)
Arzachel (one of the moon's craters)
Astron (Gr., star)
Auriga (constellation, the Charioteer)

Aurora Borealis (Northern Lights)

Bellatrix (star in Orion)
Betelgeux (reddish star in Orion)
Boötes (constellation, the Herdsman)

Callisto (satellite of Jupiter)
Camelopardalis (constellation, the Giraffe)
Canopus (2nd-brightest star in the sky)
Capella (yellow star)
Carina (constellation, part of Argo, the Keel)
Cassini (French astronomer)
Catharina (one of the moon's craters)
Celeste (Lat., heavenly)
Centaurus (constellation containing the 3rd-brightest star in the sky)
Clavius (one of the moon's craters)
Columba (constellation, the Dove)
Comet
Copernicus (Polish astronomer)
Cygnus (constellation, the Swan)

Delphinus (constellation, the Dolphin)
Dione (satellite of Saturn)
Draco (constellation, the Dragon)
Dubhe (yellow star in the Big Dipper)

Eclipse
Enceladus (satellite of Saturn)
Eridanus (constellation, the River)
Etoile (Fr., star)

Fornax (constellation, the Furnace)

Galaxy
Galileo (Italian astronomer)
Ganymede (satellite of Jupiter, yellowish)
Gegenshein (faint or diffuse glow)
Giacobbine-Zimmer (a comet)
Gibbous (a three-quarter moon)
Giordano Bruno (one of the moon's craters)
Grimaldi (one of the moon's craters)

Halley's Comet
Hesperus (evening star, Venus)
Hester (Pers., star)

Hipparchus (great plain of the
    moon; ancient Greek astronomer)
Hyperion (moon of Saturn)

Isaac Newton (English astronomer)

Kukarkin (Russian astronomer)

Leonid (shower of meteors)
Luna (Lat., moon)
Lunik (first Russian rocket series)
Lynx (constellation)

Mankarlina (star)

Merak (star in the Big Dipper)
Milky Way
Mimas (satellite of Saturn)
Mira (red star)

Nereid (satellite of Neptune)
Nostradamus (French astrologer and prophet)
Nunki (star)

Orion (constellation)

Palomar (observatory in California)
Para Selene (bright moonlike spot; mock moon)
Parhelion (bright spot on a solar halo; mock sun)
Penumbra (partial shadow outside an eclipse's
    total shadow)
Perigee (closest point to the earth in a heavenly
    body's orbit)
Perihelion (closest point to the sun in a heavenly
    body's orbit)
Peterius (one of the moon's craters)
Phoenix (constellation)
Piccolomini (one of the moon's craters)
Pleiades (the 7 Sisters, group of stars in Taurus)

Polaris (the North Star)
Primum Mobile (Lat., first moving thing; Ptolemy's
    boundary of creation)
Ptolemy (ancient Egyptian astronomer)

QSO (quasi-stellar object)
Quasar (quasi-stellar objects that appear to be
    bluish stars)

Riccioli (one of the moon's craters)
Rigel (very bright white star in Orion)

Sagitta (constellation, the Arrow)
Saros (the cycle in which eclipses occur)
Scutum (constellation, the Shield)
Sirius (brightest star, white)
Spica (white star in Virgo)
Sputnik (Russian spacecraft)

Taruntius (one of the moon's craters)
Theophilus (one of the moon's craters)
Trifid (glowing nebula, cloud of gas)
Triton (satellite of Neptune)
Tycho (moon crater; Danish astronomer)

Umbriel (satellite of Uranus)
Urania (Greek muse of astronomy)

Vega (5th-brightest star, blue-white)
Vendelinus (one of the moon's craters)
Vesper (evening star, Venus)

Wezea (star)

Yerkes (University of Chicago observatory)

Zodiac
Zozma (star)

Pairs:

Castor (white star) & Pollux (orange star)

Deimos & Phobus (moons of Mars)
Helios & Selene (sun & moon)

Biblical

Abbaddon (angel of the bottomless pit)
Abra (favorite concubine of Solomon)
Absalom (King David's favorite son)
Ahab (king of Israel, Jezebel's husband)
Ahasuerus (Persian king, husband of Queen Esther)
Amen
Apocalypse (last book of the New Testament)
Apocrypha (early writings of questionable authenticity)
Ariel (another name for Jerusalem)

Barabbas (thief released in place of Jesus)
Bartholomew (disciple of Jesus)
Bathsheba (wife of David, mother of Solomon)
Belshazzar (king of Babylon)
Bethany (town near Jerusalem)
Bethesda (pool with healing powers in ancient Jerusalem)

Corinthians (book of the New Testament)

Deuteronomy (5th book of the Old Testament)
Didymus (Thomas the Apostle)
Dorcas (woman who sewed for the poor)

Ebenezer (memorial thanking God for helping defeat the Philistines)
Ecclesiastes (book of the Old Testament)
Eden (paradise)
Elijah (Hebrew prophet)
Enoch (Cain's eldest son, father of Methuselah)
Ephesians (book of the New Testament)
Epiphany (manifestation of divine being; sudden perception)
Exodus (2nd book of the Old Testament; departure of the Jews from Egypt)
Ezekiel (Hebrew prophet)
Ezra (Hebrew scribe)

Gabriel (angel of comfort and good news)
Gallio (an indifferent official)
Gamaliel (the apostle Paul)

Genesis (1st book of the Old Testament)
Gideon (one of the judges of Israel)
Goshen (land of plenty)

Habakkuk (prophet)
Herodias (queen who caused the death of John
the Baptist)
Hezekiah (king of Judah who tried to abolish
idolatry)
Hosannah

Isaiah (greatest Hebrew prophet)
Ishmael (one at war with society)

Jeremiah (prophet; pessimist)
Jezebel (shameless, wicked wife)
Joab (commander of King David's army)
Job (personification of patience)
Jonah (Hebrew prophet)
Josiah (king of Judah)

Lazarus (brother of Mary, raised from the dead by
Jesus)
Levi (Hebrew prophet)

Leviticus (3rd book of the Old Testament)
Lilith (Talmudists' name for Adam's consort before
Eve; night monster and seducer)

Maccabaeus (ancient family that fought for Jewish
independence)
Maimonides (Hebrew philosopher)
Malachi (book of prophecy in the Old Testament)
Methuselah (oldest man in the Bible, 969 years)
Moses

Nazareth (village where Jesus lived)
Nebuchadnezzar (Assyrian king)
Nehemiah (book of the Old Testament)
Nicodemus (Pharisee who visited Jesus)
Nineveh (ancient wicked city)
Noah

Obadiah (prophet)

Pater Noster (The Lord's Prayer)
Pentateuch (1st 5 books of the Old Testament)
Philemon (book of New Testament written by Paul)
Potiphar (Joseph's master in Egypt)

Raphael (healing angel; symbolized carrying a fish)

Samaria (biblical town)
Sardius (precious stone in breastplates of Jewish high priests)
Sennacherib (Assyrian king)
Simon (apostle)
Solomon (wisest king of Israel)

Tohubohu (chaos, confusion)

Vashti (Hebrew queen)

Zacheus (small man who climbed a tree so he could see Jesus pass)
Zechariah (Hebrew prophet)
Zedekiah (king of Judah)
Zephaniah (prophet)

Pairs & Trios:

Adam & Eve
Cain & Abel
Dan & Beersheba (from one end of a place to another)
David & Bathsheba
Jacob & Esau (twin sons of Isaac and Rebecca)

Joshua & Jedidiah (dissimilar brothers)
Melchior, Gaspar & Balthazar (the 3 Magi)
Samson & Delilah
Shadrach, Meshach & Abednego
Sodom & Gomorrah

Black Magic

Abracadabra
Alakazam
Alfar (Nordic elf)
Alviss (Nordic dwarf)
Asmodeus (king of demons)
Ayesha (African immortal sorceress)

Balisarda (magical sword)
Beelzebub (Hebrew, prince of devils)
Befana (Ital., good fairy)
Belial (Hebrew, devil)

Cagliostro (Italian impostor who posed as an alchemist)
Casmira (mystic, from Voltaire's *Candide*)
Cassandra (having the gift of prophecy)
Cattywampas (destructive hobgoblin; diagonally askew)
Cleromancy (divination by throwing dice or lots)
Clidomancy (divination by means of a key)
Cloot, Clootie (Scottish, devil)
Cluricaune (Irish, elf)

Dahak (Pers., Satan)
Deva (Pers., demon)
Diablo (Span., Devil)
Doppelganger (ghostly double)
Dybbuk (Heb., mysterious, possessive spirit)

Erzulie (Haitian voodoo love goddess)
Excalibur (King Arthur's magic sword)

Fata Morgana (mirage)

Gandalf (Tolkien's wizard)
Genie
Gloriana (Spenser's *Faerie Queene*)
Gri-Gri (African lucky charm)
Grimalkin (the Devil's cat)

Hecate (queen of witches; Greek goddess of
    infernal regions)
Houdini

Jinx

Kachina (Hopi Indian spirit doll)

Karnack (mind reader)

Legerdemain (sleight-of-hand, tricks of illusion)
Lucifer (the Devil)

Malagigi (Italian magician)
Manitou (American Indian Great Spirit)
Medusa (Greek gorgon with hair of snakes)
Mephistopheles (the Devil)
Merlin
Mesmer (hypnotist)
Morgan le Fay (evil fairy; King Arthur's half-sister)

Nemesis (Greek goddess of inevitable fate)
Nibelung (dwarf who had a ring with magic
    powers)
Nissa (Scandinavian elf)
Nostradamus (prophet)

Ouija (WEE-ja, board game where players are
    guided by spirits moving a pointer)

Pandemonium (abode of all demons)
Pixie (sprite or fairy)

Poltergeist (mischievous spirit)
Pooka (Irish evil spirit)

Rahu (Hindu demon that causes eclipses)
Raksha (Hindu spirit that assumes different
    shapes)
Rasputin (Russian monk)

Shaitan (Arabic, Devil)
Shaman
Sibyl (prophetess or fortune-teller)
Svengali (hypnotist)

Taboo
Tarot
Titania (queen of fairies, *A Midsummer Night's
    Dream*, Shakespeare)

Walpurgisnacht (nickname Val; witches' sabbath)
Warlock (male witch)
Will-o'-the-Wisp (light that lures people into the
    marsh)
Wizard

Zombie

Pairs:

Abra & Cadabra
Harum & Scarum

Heebie & Jeebie
Mumbo & Jumbo

Business & Finance

Adam Smith (economist)
Agio (premium paid in exchange of foreign
    currencies)
Amex (American Stock Exchange)
Arbitrage (buy and sell stocks simultaneously)
Audit

Babbitt (Sinclair Lewis' typical businessman)
Baruch (financial wizard)
Blue Chip (outstandingly worthwhile investment)
Borsa (Italian stock exchange)
Bottom Line (profit or loss figure)
Bourse (French stock exchange)
Brassage (government fee for converting bullion
    into coins)
Buttonwood (tree under which New York Stock
    Exchange was started)

Carnegie (famed industrialist)
Caveat Emptor (Lat., let the buyer beware)
C.D. (Certificate of Deposit)

Collateral
Comex (Commodity Exchange)
Conglomerate

Debenture
De Mandeville (economist)
Dinar (coin)
Disagio (fee for exchanging depreciated foreign
    currency)
Dooteroomus (slang, money)
Dow Jones
Du Pont (famed industrialist)

Econometrics
Entrepreneur
Escrow (deposit in trust pending fulfillment of
    condition)
Eurodollar

Fannie Mae (Federal National Mortgage
    Association)

Fiduciary (holding in trust, based on confidence for value)

FIFO (first in—first out, accounting principle)

Fiscal

Forbes (financial magazine)

Freddie Mac (Federal Home Loan Mortgage Corporation)

Freddie Mae (Federal National Mortgage Association)

Fugio Cent (first coin officially used by U.S. Government, 1787)

Galbraith (economist)

Ginnie Mae (Government National Mortgage Association)

GNP (Gross National Product)

Granville (technical analyst)

Greenback

Gresham (economist who theorized, "Bad money drives out good")

Guesstimate (estimate based on conjecture)

John Maynard Keynes (economist)

J. P. Morgan (financier)

Keogh (pension plan for business owners and self-employed)

Kondatrieff (long-range economic cycle, 54–60 years)

Laffer (supply-side economist, Laffer curve)

Laissez-Faire (government noninterference in economic matters)

LIFO (last in—first out, accounting principle)

Lombard (banker or moneylender)

Ma Bell

Maggie Mae (MGIC Mortgage Marketing)

Malthus (economist)

Manny Hanny (Manufacturers Hanover Trust Company)

Maynard Keynes (economist)

Mazuma (slang, money)

M.B.A. (Master of Business Administration)

Megabucks

Mogul

Monkey Ward (nickname for Montgomery Ward)

Moody's (bond-rating service)

Moola (slang, money)

Nabob (very rich man)
NASDAQ (National Association of Security Dealers
　Automated Quotation)
No-Load (no sales fee, as on mutual funds)

Odd Lot (less than 100 shares of stock)
Option (right to buy or sell a specific stock for a
　specific price at a specific time)

Pareto (economic law of income distribution)
Payout (dividend)
Penny Ante
Penny Mae (PMI Mortgage Co.)
Penny Stock (valued at less than $1)
Perquisite (Perk)
Portfolio
Prospectus (preliminary statement to attract
　investors)
Proxy

Quotron (electronic stock-quotation system)

Raider (company that attempts to take over
　another company)

Rally
RIF (reduction in force, personnel cutback due to
　budgetary cuts or political change)
Rockefeller (world's first billionaire)
Rothschild (French tycoon)

Sally Mae (Student Loan Marketing Association)
Scruples
Shareholder
Simoleon (slang, dollar)
Sonymac (State of New York Mortgage Agency)
Spondulix (slang, cash)
Stagflation (stagnant economy & inflation)
Sterling
Straddle (buy in one market and sell in another for
　profit)

Takeover
T-Bill (Treasury bill)
Tender Offer
Thorstein Veblen (economist)
Tipster
Trader
Tycoon

Uptick (stock-market high)

Yenom (money spelled backward)

Pairs & Trios:

Atchison, Topeka & Santa Fe
Chesapeake & Ohio
Debit & Credit
Dollars & Cents
Dow & Jones
Dun & Bradstreet

Hertz & Avis
Pitman & Gregg
Put & Call
Thank You & Paine Webber
Visa & Carte Blanche
Wheeler & Dealer

Gold and Silver Coins

Bezant (Byzantine)

Chervontsi (Russian)
Cobang (Japanese)
Crusado (Portugese)

Denarius (ancient Roman)
Doubloon (Spanish)
Ducat (European)

Florin (Florentine)

Krugerrand

Louis d'Or (French)

Satang (Siamese, bronze)
Scudo (Italian)
Shekel (Biblical)

Celebrated Cats

Reynard the Fox, Aesop	Tybert
Alice's Adventures in Wonderland, Lewis Carroll	Dinah, Kitty, Snowdrop
Old Possum's Book of Practical Cats, T. S. Eliot	Asparagus, Bustopher Jones, Coricopat, Firefrorefiddle, Grizabella, Growltiger, Grumbuskin, Jellylorum, Jennyanydots, Macavity, Mr. Mistoffelees, Mungojerrie, Munkustrap, Lady Griddlebone, Old Deuteronomy, Quaxo, Rumpleteazer, Rumpuscat, Rum Tum Tugger, Skimbleshanks, Tumblebrutus
Paul Gallico	Thomasina, Tough Tom, Tough Charlie
The Owl and the Pussycat, Edward Lear	Chessy, Foss
Don Marquis	Mehitabel
The House at Pooh Corner, A. A. Milne	Tigger
Ovid	Galanthis (red cat)

Beatrix Potter	Tabitha Twitchit, Tom Kitten
Peter and the Wolf, Prokofiev	Ivan
Saki's talking cat	Tobermory
The King of Cats, B. Sleigh	Carbonel
Booth Tarkington	Gypsy
Mark Twain	Beelzebub, Buffalo Bill, Cataline, Cataraugus, Catasaugua, Tom Quartz
Bell, Book and Candle, John Van Druten	Pyewacket
The Malediction, Tennessee Williams	Mitchevo
The Cat and the Moon, William Butler Yeats	Minnaloushe
Agatha Christie	Wonky Poo

Celebrities' Cats

Jack Albertson	Tara, Tut-Azam
Cleveland Amory	Annabelle, Benedict
Matthew Arnold	Atossa (Toss)
Russell Baker	Alcibiades, Son
George Balanchine	Mourka (Rus., purr)
Tallulah Bankhead	Dolly
Clive Barnes	Candy Cane, Apricot
Richard Basehart	Black Kitty, Noel
Barbara Baxley	Mr. Fay Wray, Isabel, Tula
Valerie Bertinelli	Tuxedo
Alexander Borodin	Rybolov (Rus., fisherman), Dlinyenki
Ray Bradbury	Nutty
Jimmy Breslin	Kitty
Emily Brontë	Tom
Helen Gurley Brown	Samantha
Rita Mae Brown	Baby Jesus
Ellen Burstyn	Moses, Georgia Baby
Red Buttons	Tiggy
Roger Caras	Rufus, Daisy, Mr. Amanda, Fidel

Thomas Carlyle	Columbine
John Carradine	Howja, Leika
Keith Carradine	Mouse, Pumpkin
Lewis Carroll	Dinah
Amy Carter	Mister Malarky Ying Yang
Rosemary Casals	Cat
Peggy Cass	Alice
Carol Channing	Geewhiz
Winston Churchill	Jock
Georges Clemenceau	Prudence
Imogene Coca	Gainzer, David Garrick I and II
Jean Cocteau	Franchette, Saha, Zwerg, Sido, Chartreaux, La Chatte Dernière
Franco Columbu (Mr. Universe)	Angel
Walter Cronkite	Dancer
Gloria DeHaven	Leo, Daisy, Duke, Curtis
Colleen Dewhurst	Tinker Two, Tiger, Vivian, Juanita, Barney, Marvin (after Marvin Gardens in Monopoly)
Charles Dickens	Williamina (William until she had a litter)
Alexandre Dumas	Mysouff, Le Docteur
Albert Einstein	Sizi

Barry Farber	Frankie
Roberta Flack	Caruso
Eileen Ford	Kiki
Gerald Ford	Shan
Anatole France	Hamilcar, Pascal
Anne Frank	Mouschi
Eva Gabor	Magda
Zsa Zsa Gabor	Miss Puss Puss
John Kenneth Galbraith	Gujarat
Lillian Gish	Romney, Threezy
Barry Gray	Rudi (after Nureyev), Nichevo, Miss Mangletail
Thomas Gray	Selima
Tammy Grimes	Teegy, The Peach
Bryant Gumble	Justine
Thomas Hardy	Hardy's Cat, Cobby
June Havoc	Cecil Cat, Sam Cat
Edith Head	Pussycat, Thomas Gainsborough
Lafcadio Hearn	Tama
Ernest Hemingway	Cuba, Crazy Christian, Friendless' Brother, Ecstasy
Vladimir Horowitz	Bigia
Victor Hugo	Chanoine (or Gavroche)
Robert Indiana	Peteepeeto

Henry James	Princess
Samuel Johnson	Hodge, Lily
Shirley Jones	Rebel
James Jones	Ramses, Danielle of Memphis
Bel Kaufman	Annie Arbor
Lainie Kazan	Blossom, Prinderella, Romeo and Juliet
Michael Korda	Queenie
Edward Lear	Foss
Jerry Lewis	Pussycat
Abe Lincoln's son Tad	Tabby
John MacDonald	Amazin' Grace
Steve Martin	Dr. Carlton B. Forbes
James Mason	Tree, Topboy, Whitey, Lady Leeds, Spring
Mary McFadden	Zinzar (after the town in Rhodesia)
Ed McMahon	Hershey Bar, Queen Tut, W. C. Fields, Colonel Montezuma
	Black Beau
Lee Merriwether	Muezza
Mohammed	Shall, Will
Christopher Morley	Solomon
Jan Morris	
Louise Nevelson	Raggedy Ann

Jane Pauley	Meatball
Edgar Allan Poe	Catarina
Pope Leo XII	Micetto
Juliet Prowse	Puddy
Queen Victoria	White Heather
Dan Rather	Geronimo
Cardinal Richelieu	Gazette, Lucifer, Ludovic le Cruel
Nan Robertson	Kate, William
Kenny Rogers	Kit and Caboodle
Theodore Roosevelt	Slippers, Tom Quartz
Christina Rossetti	Grimalkin
Vincent Sardi	Jerry, Twinkles
Dick Schaap	Gandhi
Sir Walter Scott	Hinse of Hinsefield
Tom Seaver	Ferguson (Jenkins, the pitcher)
Edie Sedgwick	Smoke
Gene Shalit	Junior
Liz Smith	Suzanne, Mr. Ships
Stevie Smith	Tizdal
Suzanne Somers	Tom
David Susskind	Oliver

William Makepeace Thackeray
Henry David Thoreau
Mark Twain

Louis Untermeyer

Brenda Vaccaro
Frankie Valli
Gwen Verdon

Betsy von Furstenberg

Nancy Walker
Horace Walpole
Dennis Weaver
H. G. Wells
Tom Wicker
Harold Wilson
Gretchen Wyler

Louisa
Min
Sour Mash, Apollinaris, Zarathustra, Zoroaster,
   Blatherskite

Missy Potato, Bobo, Locket, Plush, Cleopatra,
   Flaccus, Tiger Lily

Chauncy, China
Christopher, Alison
Daisy, Super Cat, Fatrick, Feets Fosse, Tumbler
   Fosse, Junie Moon
Minou

Lump
Selima, Zara, Patapan, Harold
Ringo
Mr. Peter Wells
Colonel
Nemo
Sweet Charity, Shadow

Children's Names & Comics

Aladdin
Alfred E. Neuman
Alley Oop
Amscray (Pig Latin, scram)
Artoo Deetoo
Aslan (C. S. Lewis' talking lion)

Barney Rubble
Bazooka
Betty Boop
Bingo
Bit o' Honey
Blackbeard
Bluebeard
Bobbsey
Bo Peep
Bozo
Buck Rogers
Buster Brown

Captain Kangaroo

Captain Kidd
Captain Kirk
Cartwheel
Carvel
Casper (the Friendly Ghost)
Charade
Charlie Brown
Cheerios
Chuckles
Cinderella
Colonel Sanders
Conan
Cookie
Count Chocula
Cracker Jack
Crayola
Cubbins (Dr. Seuss character)
Cupcake
Curious George

Davy Crockett

Deely Bobber
Domino
Dondi
Dr. Denton
Dr. Doolittle
Dr. Seuss
Dunkin Donut
Dyn-O-Mite

Elmer Fudd
Ernie
E.T.

Fearless Fosdick (*Dick Tracy* character)
Felix
Figaro (Pinocchio's cat)
Fig Newton
Firefly
Flash Gordon
Flubber
Fluffernutter
Frankenberry
Frère Jacques
Friar Tuck (*Robin Hood*)

Friday (Robinson Crusoe's friend)
Frisbie
Frito
Fritzi Ritz
Frodo Baggins (*Lord of the Rings,* Tolkien)
Froot Loops
Fussbudget

Galoshes
Gangbusters
Garfield
Georgie Porgie
Gepetto (Pinocchio's father)
Gerald McBoing-Boing
Gingersnap
Goldilocks
Goober
Goody-Two-Shoes
Gravel Gertie (*Dick Tracy* character)
Greedo
Gremlin
Grinch (Dr. Seuss character)
Gulliver
Gumbie
Gumdrop

Heidi
Hiawatha
Hobbit (*Lord of the Rings,* Tolkien)
Hokey Pokey
Hop o' My Thumb
Hopscotch

Howdy Doody
Humpty Dumpty

Jack Horner
Jack Sprat
Jellybean
Jiminy Cricket

Katzen Jammer
Kazootie
Kitchy-Koo
Kris Kringle
Krypton (Superman's planet)

Lego
Lex Luther (villain in *Superman*)
Little John (*Robin Hood*)
Long John Silver (*Treasure Island,* Stevenson)
Loony Tunes
Lord Fauntleroy

Macaroni
Madam Purrtwitchet
Malomar

Mandrake the Magician
Marco Polo
Mary Poppins
Marzipan
McMuffin
Minnehaha ("Laughing Water," *Hiawatha,*
    Longfellow)
Miss Muffet
Miss Peach
Miss Purrington
Miss Spoonatuna
Mr. Greenjeans
Mr. Magoo
Mrs. Sippy
Moby Dick
Monty Python
Moppet
Mother Goose
Mother Hubbard
Mumbletypeg
Munchkin
Muppet

Narnia (C. S. Lewis)

Neat-O
Nokomis (daughter of the moon, *Hiawatha,*
    Longfellow)

O. Henry
Olive
Oreo
Oz

Pablum
   Pac-Man
      Paddington
         Peanut Butter
            Peekaboo
               Peppermint Patty
               Peter Pan
         Pickles
      Pinocchio
Pippi Longstocking
Pizza Pie
Pocahontas
Pogo
Poindexter
Pollyanna

Pom Pom
Popcorn
Prince Charming
Prince Valiant
Puff

Rapunzel
Riki Tiki Tavi (*Jungle Books,* Kipling)
Rip Van Winkle
Robin Hood
Robinson Crusoe
Rubba Dub Dub
Rumpelstiltskin

Shmoo (*Li'l Abner* creature)
Scrabble
Shazam
Sheena (Queen of the Jungle)
Sir Lancelot
Skeezix
Smurf
Snickers
Snow White
Somersault

Sparkle Plenty (*Dick Tracy* character)
Strawberry Shortcake
Stuart Little
Swee' Pea
Sylvester

Tapioca
Tar Baby
Tarzan
Tattletail
Thumbelina
Tiddlywinks
Tigger
Tinker Bell
Tiny Tim
Tom Thumb
Tonka
Tootsie Roll
Topsy Turvy
Tweety Pie
Twinkie

Uncle Remus
Uncle Wiggily

Vitamin Flintheart (*Dick Tracy* character)

Wee Willie Winkie
Whirligig
Wigglesworth
Willie Wonka
Wimpy
Winnie the Pooh

Winnie Winkle
Wooki

Yodel
Yoo Hoo
Yo-Yo

Zwieback

Pairs & Trios

Barnum & Bailey
Batman & Robin
Blondie & Dagwood
Celeste & Babar
Chitty Chitty & Bang Bang
Daddy Warbucks & Orphan Annie
Dick Tracy & Tess Trueheart
Eeny Meeny & Miny Mo
Hansel & Gretel
Heidi & Peter
Hickory, Dickory & Dock
Ignatz & Krazy Kat
Ken & Barbie

Kukla, Fran & Ollie
Li'l Abner & Daisy Mae
Maggie & Jiggs
Mutt & Jeff
Olive Oyl & Popeye
Pebbles & Bam Bam
Ping & Pong
Puss & Boots
Tom & Jerry
Tom Sawyer & Huckleberry Finn
Tweedledum & Tweedledee
Wynken, Blynken & Nod
Yankee, Doodle & Dandy

Computers

Adabas (computer language)

Babbage (father of computer technology)

Cobol (Common Ordinary Business-Oriented Language)

Digibyte (computer software company)
Dinabyte (minicomputer)

Fortran (computer language)
Fosdic (scanning device)

GIGO (garbage in/garbage out)
Glitch (source of a malfunction)

Hal (*2001*)

Lady Lovelace (computer language)

Mumps (computer language)

Pascal (computer language)
Pixel (computer language)

Shockley (inventor of the transistor)
Silicon (computer chip)

TAT (turnaround time)

Cowboys & Indians

Alamo
Apache
Appomattox
Argonaut (person who went West during the Gold
    Rush)
Autry

Bat Masterson
Belle Starr
Billy the Kid
Bowie
Brigham Young
Buckaroo
Buffalo Bill

Cactus Pete
Cherokee
Cheyenne
Chickahominy
Chickamauga
Chickasaw

Choctaw
Colonel Cody
Comanche
Conestoga
Cumberland
Custer

Dale Evans
Desperado
Destry
Doc Holliday

Gabby Hayes
Geronimo

Hoot Gibson
Hopalong Cassidy
Hud

Iroquois

Jackeroo (cowboy)
Jesse James
J.R. (*Dallas*)

Kickapoo (Algonquin Indian; means "He stands
    out")
Kit Dalton (outlaw)

Lariat
Leni-Lenape (Delaware Indians)
Lone Ranger
Lone Star
Louis L'Amour

Ma Barker
Marshal Dillon
Maverick (loner)
Mesquite

Paladin
Pawnee
Pogamoggan (Indian war club)
Ponderosa

Remington
Roy Rogers

Sachem (tribal chief)
Shane
Shawnee
Sheriff
Sheriff Lobo
Shoshone
Sombrero
Susquehanna

Tallahatchie
Tecumseh (Indian chief)
Tex Ritter (movie actor in Westerns)
Thataway
Tom Mix
Tonto
Trigger
Tumbleweed

Wampum
Will Rogers

Winchester
Wyatt Earp

Zane Grey

Butch Cassidy & The Sundance Kid
Lone Ranger & Tonto

Pairs:
Roy Rogers & Dale Evans

Dance

Adagio
Alvin Ailey
Arabesque

Baborak (Bohemian national dance)
Balanchine
Baryshnikov
Bojangles
Bolshoi
Bossanova

Can-Can
Capezio

Diaghilev
Disco
Do-Si-Do

Eglevsky
Entrechat

Fandango (lively Spanish dance)
Farandole (lively dance of Provence, France)
Farruca (Gypsy dance)
Furlana (Venetian gondoliers' dance)

Hepcat
Hokey Pokey
Hootchie Cootchie
Hully-Gully

Isadora Duncan

Jacques D'Amboise
Joffrey

Kazatsky (Russian dance step)

Limbo
Lindy Hop
Lola Falana

Markova
Maxixe (ma-SHE-shay, Brazilian dance)
Mazurka

Nijinsky
Nureyev

Pas de Deux (ballet for 2 dancers)
Pas de Trois (ballet for 3 dancers)
Paso Doble (bullfight music)
Pavlova
Petrouchka (ballet)
Pilobolus (dance theater group)
Pirouette (spinning around on one foot)
Polka
Polonaise (stately promenade)
Pousette (dancing around with joined hands)
Pulcinella (Stravinsky ballet)

Quadrille (square dance)

Buck & Bubbles
Busby & Berkeley

Rockette
Roland Petit
Ruby Keeler
Rumba

Saltarello (Spanish and Italian dance like a jig)
Saraband (slow, stately Spanish dance)
Sir Roger de Coverley (English country dance, like a Virginia reel)
Sirtaki (Greek dance)
Spoleto (Italian dance-festival site)

Tarantella (Italian dance)
Tedesca (German dance)
Terpsichore (terp-SIC-o-ree, Greek muse of the dance)
Trocadero (ballet company from Monte Carlo)
Tutu
Twyla Tharp

Pairs:

Fred & Ginger

Detectives & Villains

Charlie Chan

Dr. No

Ellery Queen
Ernst Stavro Blofeld

Father Brown

Gumshoe

Hercule Poirot
Hugo Drax

Inspector Clouseau (*The Pink Panther*)
Inspector Maigret

James Bond

Lord Peter Wimsey

Mannix
McCloud

McGarret
Mickey Spillane
Mike Hammer
Miss Marple
Mr. Moto
Mouchard (Fr., police spy)

Nancy Drew
Nero Wolfe
Nick Carter

Odd Job

Philo Vance

Nick & Nora Charles

Professor Moriarty
Pussy Galore

Rex Stout
Rosa Klebb

Sam Spade
Scaramanga (James Bond villain)
Sergeant Cribb
Serpico
Shamus (slang, detective)
Sherlock Holmes

Whodunit

Pairs:

Sherlock Holmes & Dr. Watson

Exotic Breeds

Abacus (Chinese hand calculator using beads)
Abdullah
Aga Khan
Agni (Hindu deity)
Aisha (favorite wife of Mohammed)
Akbar (Indian emperor)
Aladdin
Ali Baba
Al Sirat (the *Koran;* "the right way")
Amahl (Menotti's opera)
Amaterasu (Shinto sun goddess)
Amida (Buddhist god of light)
Amon (Egyptian god)
Anubis (Egyptian conductor of the dead in the
    netherworld)
Atari
Attila
Azuki (Jap., red bean, means good health)

Babouche (slipper worn in Iran)
Baghdad

Bahadur (Anglo-Indian, distinguished personage)
Baksheesh (tip or bribe in Middle East)
Banzai (Jap., "May you live 10,000 years")
Baraka (Arabic, being blessed and blessing)
Batik (wax technique of dying fabric)
Bokhara (Arab rug)
Bombay
Bonsai (miniature Japanese trees)
Botacha (Hindi, "certainly yes")
Brahma (Hindu creator)
Buddha
Bwana (Swahili, master)
Byzantium (ancient name of Constantinople)

Caliph (head of Moslem state)
Cathay
Chandra (Sansk., moonlike)
Charlie Chan
Confucius
Cyrus (Pers., sun)

Darjeeling (delicate Indian tea)
Dashahara (Indian festival)
Désirée
Devi (Hindu goddess)
Dhurrie (Indian rug)
Durga (Hindu goddess, representing female
    energy)

Effendi (Arabic title of respect)
Euphrates

Farah
Faridun (legendary Persian king)
Farouk (Egyptian king)
Fatima
Fuchi (Japanese fire goddess)
Fudo (Japanese god of wisdom)
Fuji (Japanese mountain)
Fu Manchu

Gamel(a) (Arabic, beautiful)
Gandhi
Ganesha (gan-AY-sha, Hindu god of success and
    wisdom)

Geisha
Genghis Khan
Ginseng (root with medicinal properties)
Gobi (desert)
Gunga Din (Indian water carrier, Kipling)
Guru (Indian teacher, wise man)

Haiku (Japanese poetic form)
Hammurabi (Babylonian emperor)
Hapi (Egyptian god of the Nile)
Harpocretes (Egyptian god of silence)
Hatshepsut (Egyptian queen)
How-Too (Chinese earth-monster god)
Hussein

Ichibon (Jap., number one)
Indra (Hindu deity)
Ishtar (Babylonian love goddess)
Isis (Egyptian goddess identified with the moon)

Jaipur (city in India)
Jamshid (Persian mythical fairy king)
Joss (Chinese god of luck)

Kabuki (classical Japanese dramatic dance)
Kaffiyeh (Arab headdress)
Kahawa (Swahili, coffee)
Kakemono
   (Japanese
   painting
   mounted
   on a
   roller)

Kali (Hindu goddess)
Kalinda (Sansk., sun)
Kalinga (ancient kingdom of India)
Kalki (liberator)
Kama (Hindu god of love)
Kamaria (African, moonlike)
Karma
Kashan
Katmandu
Katouki (Greek bistro)
Kawasaki
Kepi (Arab cap)
Khisu (Korean, miracle worker)
King Tsu (Chin., Confucius)
Kira (Pers., sun)
Kismet (fate)
Koto (Japanese stringed instrument)
Krishna (Hindu god of fire, lightning, heaven and
   the sun)
Kshatriya (Indian warrior class)
Kubera (Hindu god of wealth)
Kublai Khan (Mongol emperor of China, grandson
   of Genghis Khan)
Kuro (Hindu prince)

Layla (Arabic, dark as night)
Li Po (Chinese poet)

Maharajah (Indian ruler)
Maharani (wife of Indian ruler)
Mahatma (Sansk., great soul)
Mah Jong (Chinese game)
Maiko (MY-ko, Japanese girl training to be a
    geisha)
Manchu (Chinese dynasty)
Mandala (Buddhist symbol of meditation)
Mantra (Hindu prayer; instrument of thought)
Manu (Hindu father of the human race)
Marabout (Moslem holy man)
Mariko
Mata Hari
Michiko
Midas (legendary king with a golden touch)
Ming (Chinese dynasty)
Mirza (Iranian title of honor; royal prince)
Momus (Greek god of sleep and dreams)

Nawob (Moslem title giving princely status)
Nefertiti (Egyptian queen)

Nehru
Nirvana (Buddhist ideal of heavenly peace)
Nogaku (Japanese classical dramatic dance)
Nunchaku (karate technique)

Obi (Japanese sash)
Odalisque (Turkish harem slave)
Odessa
Omar Khayyam
Origami (Japanese art of paper folding)
Osiris (Egyptian god)

Pachinko (Japanese pinball game)
Pango-Pango
Pan-Ku (Chinese legendary giant whose body
    formed the world)
Peri (Pers., beautiful spirit)
Pongee (silk)
Punjab

Quivara (mythical city of treasures)

Rajpat (Indian ruling class)
Rama (Hindi, joy bringer)

Rani (Sansk., queen, wife of the rajah)
Rawalpindi (Pakistani city)
Rubáiyát (Omar Khayyam)

Sabu (1940s Indian movie actor)
Sadi (Persian poet)
Safari
Saladin (Egyptian sultan)
Samarkand
Samisen (Japanese geisha's guitarlike instrument)
Sampan (Chinese boat)
Sarouk (Arab rug)
Satori (Buddhist state of spiritual enlightenment)
Scheherazade
Sepoy (anglicized form of Hindu "sipaki," soldier)
Shah Jahan (Indian emperor, "King of the World")
Shakti (Hindu state of spiritual enlightenment;
    female energy)
Shamash (Babylonian sun god)
Shami (Arab., pomegranate)
Shangri-La
Shang-Ti (Chinese god of heaven)
Sheba
Shikari (native guide or hunter in India)

Shogun
Shoji (Japanese screen)
Siam
Simba
Sindbad
Siva (Hindu god, the destroyer)
Sri Lanka
Suleiman
Suntory
Surya (Hindi deity)
Suzuki
Swami

Tabriz (Arab rug)
Taching (Da-ching, Manchu dynasty)
Taj Mahal
Tamerlane (ancient Tartar conqueror; also
    Tamburlaine)
Tarakee (legendary Brahmin ascetic)
Taras Bulba (15th-century Cossack)
Tarboosh (Arab hat)
Tarquin (legendary Etruscan king)
Tiki (Polynesian god)
Timbuktu
Tinar (Etruscan fire god)
Tojo (Japanese general)
Trimurti (Sansk., having 3 forms)
Typhon (Egyptian god)

Ultima Thule (distant, unknown region)

Vidar (or Vali; Scandinavian god of silence)
Vindaloo
Vishnu (Hindu god, the preserver)
Vivehananda (Indian swami)

Xanadu (Coleridge's magical place)
Xenos (Gr., stranger)
Xerxes (Persian ruler)

Yama (Hindu deity)
Yangtze
Yenshee (residue in opium pipe)

Zen

Pairs:

Chow Mein & Lo Mein
Eng & Chang (Siamese twins)
Hara & Kiri
Lapsong & Souchong (2 kinds of tea)

Rajah & Pasha
Tigris & Euphrates
Yin & Yang (masc. & fem. symbols; earth &
    heaven)

Fashion

Adolfo
Amorini (cupid motif)
Anthemion (flat floral ornament)
Antimacassar (lace doily)
Art Deco
Art Nouveau
Aubusson

Balenciaga
Bargello
Bauble
Beau Brummel (fashion dandy of the 1800s)
Beleek (Irish fine china)
Bentley
Bermondsey (London antiques market)
Bloomingdale's
Bon Ton (Fr., good style; fashionable society)
Boucheron (Parisian jeweler)
Briolette (pear-shaped diamond)
Buccellati (Italian jeweler)
Burberry

Cabriole (curved leg)
Cadillac
Calvin Klein
Cameo
Cartier
Cartouche (shield-shaped ornament)
Cavetto (concave molding)
Charmeuse (satin)
Chichi
Christie's (auction house)
Coalport (English china)
Coco Chanel
Corbeil (flower- or fruit-basket ornament)
Coromandel (Chinese screen)
Crocket (medieval ornamental plant design)
Cullinan (largest cut diamond, in the British
    imperial scepter)

Daché
Dado (lower part of pedestal or wall)
Daimler

Duncan Phyfe (American cabinetmaker)

Eglomise (painting on glass)

Fabergé (French jewelry designer)
Farthingale (hoop skirt)
Fendi
Fichu (neck ruffle)
Fiorucci
Fouquet (Parisian confectioner)
Fresco
Frowick (Halston's last name)

Galanos
Gew Gaw
Gimcrack
Giorgio Armani
Givenchy
Godiva
Gucci
Guilloche (circular border design)

Halston
Harry Winston

Henri Bendel
Hepplewhite
Hi Tech

Jeeves
Jet Set
Jewel

Kamali
Kenzo
Koh-i-noor (diamond in the Queen Mother's crown)

Limoges
Loehmann's
Louis Quatorze (Quinze, Seize, Treize)
Louis Vuitton
Lutèce

Major Domo (in charge of the household)
Maud Frizon
Meissen (German china)
Mercedes-Benz
Missoni

Nina Ricci
Nippon

Parke Bernet (auction house)
Pentimento (painting revealed beneath another)
Per Spook (dress designer)
Peugeot
Pierre Cardin
Plantagenet (English royal family, Henry II–
    Richard III)
Porthault

Quaritch (London antique-book store)
Queen Anne

Repoussé (ornament with raised design in relief)
Rolls-Royce

Scalamandrè
Schiaparelli
Sheraton (English cabinetmaker, 18th century)
Sotheby (auction house)

Taffeta
Trigère
Twiggy

Verushka

Pairs:

Abercrombie & Fitch
Fortnum & Mason
Hammacher & Schlemmer
Lord & Taylor

Neiman & Marcus
Sears & Roebuck
Statler & Hilton
Tiffany & Woolworth
Waldorf & Astoria

Flora*

Acacia
Acanthus
Agapanthus
Ailanthus
Alameda
Alyssum
Amaranth
Anemone
Arbutus
Arugula
Asphodel
Aspidistra
Aster

Basil
Begonia
Belladonna
Blossom
Bluebell

Bonsai
Buttercup

Caraway
Cardamom
Catalpa
Catananche
Celandine
Chervil
Chinquapin
Chrysanthemum
Cilantro
Clematis
Clover
Columbine
Comino (Ital., cumin)
Coriander

Daffydowndilly
Dahlia

Plants that are harmful to cats have been omitted.

Daisy
Dandelion
Dracaena

Eglantine
Eucalyptus

Floribunda
Forsythia
Frangipani
Fraxinella

Galanthus (snowdrop)
Gardenia
Ginkgo
Gladiola
Gloxinia
Goldenrod

Heather
Helianthus (sunflower)
Heliotrope
Hemlock
Hickory

Holly
Honeysuckle
Hortus Siccus (herbarium)
Huckleberry
Hyacinth

Impatiens
Ivy

Jacaranda
Japonica
Jasmine
Juniper

Kalika
Kudzu (vine considered a pest)

Larkspur
Lavender
Leilani
Leucojum
Lilac
Lily
Linnaeus (botanist who classified plants)

Lizzie-Run-in-the-Hedge
Lobelia
Loblolly
Lotus

Magnolia
Marigold
Marjoram
Mille-Fiori
Millefleurs
Mimosa
Moonflower
Morning Glory
Mulberry
Myrtle

Oregano
Osmunda

Pachysandra
Palmetto
Panax Quinquefolia (ginseng)
Pansy
Parsley

Pawpaw
Periwinkle
Petunia
Pimpernel
Poinciana
Pomona (Roman goddess of fruits)
Poppy
Portulaca
Primrose
Pussywillow

Queen Anne's Lace
Quercus

Silver Bell
Sumac
Sweetbrier
Sweet Cicely
Sweet Pea
Sweet William
Sycamore

Tamarack
Tamarisk

Tansy
Tarragon
Tiger Lily
Touch-Me-Not
Trillium
Tulip

Valerian

Verbena
Vertumnus (Roman guardian of gardens)
Vibernum

Willow
Wisteria

Zinnia

Foreign Words and Expressions

Ad Vivum (Lat., to the life)
Allez-Vous-En (Fr., go away, get out)
Amigo, Amiga (Span., friend)
Anno Domini (Lat., in the year of our Lord)
Ante Bellum (Lat., before the war, especially the
    Civil War)
Ante Meridian (Lat., before noon)
Arrondissement (subdivision in France)
Au Contraire (Fr., on the contrary)
Au Courant (Fr., well informed)

Babushka (Rus., grandmother)
Bacci (Ital., kisses)
Bagatelle (Fr., trifle)
Bambino, Bambina (Ital., baby)
Bambola (Ital., doll)
Bandido (Span., bandit)
Barbe (Ital., whiskers)
Basilikon (Gr., kingly)
Baudrons (Scottish name for a cat, like Bruin the
    bear)

Beau (Fr., handsome)
Beau Geste (Fr., gracious gesture)
Beaux Yeux (Fr., beautiful eyes)
Bel Ami (Fr., beautiful friend)
Belle (Fr., beautiful)
Bellissimo, Bellissima (Ital., most beautiful)
Benito, Benita (Lat., blessed)
Ben Trovato (Ital., happily discovered)
Bête Noire (Fr., dark beast or nemesis)
Bibi (Hindi, lady)
Billet Doux (Fr., love letter)
Bonditt (Yiddish, likable rascal)
Bonheur (Fr., happiness, good luck)
Bonhomie (Fr., good nature)
Bonito, Bonita (Span., pretty)
Bonjour (Fr., Good day)
Bonne Compagnie (Fr., good company)
Bonzer (Austral. slang, very good)
Boutonnière (Fr., lapel flower)
Boyo (Irish, lad)
Brujo, Bruja (Span., sorcerer, sorceress)

Bubeleh (Yiddish, darling)

Callestra (Gr., most beautiful)
Canajoharie (Amer. Indian, the pot that washes
    itself)
Cazar (Span., to hunt)
Chaim Yank'l (HY-em YONK-'l, Yiddish, Sad Sack)
Chatchka (Yiddish, knickknack)
Chatul (Heb., cat)
Cherchez la Femme (Fr., look for the woman)
Chéri, Chérie (Fr., loved one)
Chico, Chica (Span., small)
Chiquito, Chiquita (Span., very small)
Choux (Fr., cabbage; "mon petit choux,"
    expression of endearment)
Chutzpa (Yiddish, impudence)
Cin-Cin (cheen-cheen, Ital., a toast)
Clochard (Fr., vagabond)
Clou (Fr., the main attraction)
Con Amore (Ital., with love and tenderness)

Dakoo (Hindi, bandit)
Déjà Vu (Fr., already seen)
Dies Faustus (Lat., lucky day)

Dinkum (Aust. slang, very good)
Dolce (DAWL-chay, Ital., sweet)
Dominus Vobiscum (Lat., the Lord be with you)
Doucette (Fr., sweet one)
Dulcis (Lat., sweet)
Duniewassa (Scot., Highland gentleman)

Enfant Gâté (Fr., spoiled child)
E Pluribus Unum (Lat., one out of many)
Esprit de Corps (Fr., sense of union and
    responsibility)
Eureka (Gr., I have found it)

Far Niente (Ital., doing nothing)
Farouche (Fr., shy; also fierce)
Faux Pas (Fr., mistake)
Felina (Lat., catlike)
Felis Silvestris
    (Lat., wild cat)
Felis Viverina
    (Lat.,
    fishing cat)
Felix Culpa
    (Lat., happy fault)

Fidus Achates (Lat., trusted friend)
Fleur-de-Lis (Fr., lily-like design)

Galentine (Fr. archaic, lover)
Garçon d'Honneur (Fr., best man)
Gato, Gata (Span., cat)
Gatito, Gatita (Span., kitten)
Gattino, Gattina (Ital., kitten)
Gaucho (Span., cowboy)
Gendarme (Fr., policeman)
Gettone (Ital., telephone token)
Gordo, Gorda (Span., fat)
Gusanita (Span., little worm)

Hadji (Arab., traveler)
Hesychos (Gr., still, calm)
Hetaera (he-TAY-ra, Gr., female companion or
    mistress)
Hic et Ubique (Lat., here and everywhere)

Jamais (Fr., never)
Je Ne Sais Quoi (Fr., something inexpressible)
Je T'aime (Fr., I love you)
Joli, Jolie (Fr., pretty)

Keely (Irish, beautiful)
Kibitzer (Yiddish, busybody)
Kitzella (Yiddish, little cat)
Koshka (Rus., cat)
Koyaanisqatsi (Hopi Indian, crazy life)

L'Chaim (l'-HIGH-im, Heb., to life, a toast)

Magnus, Magna (Lat., great)
Malako (Rus., milk)
Mange-Tout (Fr., eat-everything)
Marché aux Puces (Fr., flea market)
Mavi (Armenian, lucky blue-black stone)
Mavourneen (Irish, my darling)
Maximillian (Lat., greatest male)
Maxine (Lat., greatest female)
Mea Culpa (Lat., my fault)
Micetto, Micetta (Ital., kitten)
Miciacco (mee-CHAHK-co, Ital., frisky kitten)
Micino, Micina (Ital., kitten)
Micio (MEE-cho, Ital., tomcat)
Midollo (Ital., bread crumb)
Miette (Fr., little crumb)
Mignon, Mignonne (Fr., cute)

Minette (Fr., little flirt)
Mio Gatto, Mio Gatta (Ital., my cat)
Mirabile Dictu (Lat., amazing as it may seem)
Mishugah (Miss Sugar, Yiddish, crazy)
Mitzvah (Yiddish, good deed)
Moggie (Brit. slang, cat)
Moli (Scand., crumb)
Monacello (moan-a-CHEL-lo, Ital., little monk)
Monello (Ital., brat)
Mono (Span., cute, monkey)
Morceau (Fr., small morsel)
Moto Guzzi (Ital., motorcycle)

Nemo Me Impune (Lat., nobody provokes me)
N'est-ce Pas? (Fr., Don't you agree?)
Nicht Wahr? (Ger., Isn't that right?)
Nimnochka (Rus., a little bit)
Noli Me Tangere (Lat., touch-me-not)
Nota Bene (Lat., observe what follows, take notice)
Novo, Nova (Lat., new)
Nudna (Rus., pest)
Nudnik (Yiddish, pest)
Nugae (Lat., trifles, nonsense)

Octavius, Octavia (Lat., 8th-born)
On Dit (Fr., rumor)
Orecchiette (Ital., little ears)

Papillon (Fr., butterfly)
Passim (Lat., here and there)
Pauca Verba (Lat., few words)
Pax Vobiscum (Lat., Peace be with you)
Pecoso, Pecosa (Span., freckled)
Peregrine (Lat. peregrinus, wanderer)
Piccolissimo (Ital., tiny)
Prego (Ital., Please, You're welcome)
Presto (Ital., quick)
Prima (Lat., first)
Primus/Prima Inter Pares (Lat., first among his/her
    peers)

Quiddity (Lat. quidditas, the essence)
Quidnunc (Lat., busybody)
Quintus, Quinta (Lat., 5th-born)
Qui Vive (Fr., alert)
Quizás (Span., perhaps)

Rara Avis (Lat., rarely met)

Raskolnik (Rus., dissenter)
Ravissant, Ravissante (Fr., enchanting)
Récusant, Récusante (Fr., one who refuses to
    conform)

Sal Atticus (Lat., pungent wit)
Sans Peur (sahn purr, Fr., fearless)
Sans-Souci (Fr., carefree)
Savoir-Faire (Fr., knowledge of just what to do and
    when to do it)
Savoir-Vivre (Fr., knowledge of the world, good
    breeding)
Sextus, Sexta (Lat., 6th-born)
Shabbos (Yiddish, sabbath)
Shalom (Heb., peace, hello, goodbye)
Shana (Yiddish, pretty)

Sine Qua Non (Lat., indispensable)
Sommeil (sum-MAY, Fr., sleep)
Spina (Ital., thorn)
Subito (Ital., sudden)

Tostada (Span., toast)
Toujours Gai (Fr., always merry)
Tout de Suite (toot-sweet, Fr., immediately)
Tovarich (Rus., comrade)
Tsoris (Sooris, Yiddish, trouble)
Turlupin (Fr., rascal)

Zaftig (Yiddish, juicy, plump)
Zampino (Ital., little paw)
Zeitgeist (Ger., spirit of the times)
Zoë (Gr., life)

Pairs:

Maximus & Minimus (Lat., greatest and least)
Meum & Tuum (Lat., mine and yours)
Mitten & Drinnin (Yiddish, right in the middle of
    things)

Nolens & Volens (Lat., willy-nilly)
Sturm & Drang (Ger., storm and stress)
Veni, Vidi & Vici (Lat., I came, I saw & I conquered)

Japanese

Chijo	Long life	Kuro	Black
Chika	Good Fortune		
Chocho	Butterfly	Namennayo	Don't lick me
		Nobu	Faithful
Etsu	Playful	Nyan Nyan	Meow, meow
Hana	Flower	Okin	Gold
Hoshi	Star		
		Sachiko	Joy
Jiro	2nd-born	Shinshi	Angel
Keiko	Adored	Taro	1st-born
Kimi	Sovereign (female)	Tatami	Straw mat
Kinu	Silky	Tenshi	Angel
Kiwa	Distinguished one	Tomi	Riches
Koki	Glitter	Tsuappari	Brazen
Koniko	Kitten		
Kosho	Pepper	Yuki	Lucky or snow

Chinese

Chan	Old		Li	Black
Dzi-Gin	Goodbye		Shay-Shay	Thank you
Fangtang	Lump sugar		Tang	Sugar
			Ting-Ting	Long and lasting life

If you're lucky enough to receive a cat as a gift, you might consider commemorating the occasion by naming it "Corban" (a gift to God). Or perhaps the word *gift* in a foreign language would fill the bill:

Chinese	Lee-Foo		Italian	Dono
Czech	Darek		Japanese	Okurimono
Danish	Gave (GAY-vah)		Korean	Sun Mool
Farsi	Soghati		Latin	Donum or Munus (poetical)
French	Cadeau (ca-dough)		Lithuanian	Dorte Dovena
German	Geschenk or Schenkung		Russian	Padarok
Greek	Doron		Rumanian	Cadou (ca-doo)
Hebrew	Matanah or Kishron		Spanish	Regalo (fem., Regala)
Hungarian	Agendek (i-GAN-dig)		Yiddish	Metunah

Journalists

Asterisk

Bafflegab (obfuscation)
Bagehot (English economist & editor)
Baskerville (typeface)
Benday (dots in photo-engraving)
Blickensderfer (early-1900s typewriter)
Bodoni (modern typeface)
Brenda Starr
Buchwald
By-line

Caslon (old-style typeface)
Catachresis (malapropism or mixed metaphor)
Caxton (1st English printer; also typeface)
Chancellor
Clarendon (thick, condensed typeface)
Clark Kent
Cliché
Copycat
Cronkite

Ampersand
Amphigory (nonsense writing, parody)
ASNE (American Society of Newspaper Editors)

Dingbat (typographical mark signaling an opening
    sentence or separating paragraphs)
Ditto

Elite (typeface)
Ergo
Erma Bombeck
Etaoin Shrdlu (Linotype keys, indicates an error)
Etcetera

Feuilleton (Fr., miscellaneous articles at bottom of
    newspaper pages)
Follett (writer on modern American usage)
Fowler (writer on modern English usage)
Furor Scribendi (Lat., rage for writing)

Garamond (typeface)
Gobbledygook
Godey (19th-century magazine publisher)
Grolier
Guccione
Gutenberg

Herblock

Horace Greeley
Hunter Thompson

Ibid

Jake Barnes (*The Sun Also Rises,* Hemingway)
Jargon
Jimmy Olson (*Superman*)

Kiosk
Korinna (typeface)

Lapsus Calami (Lat., slip of the pen)
Lincoln Steffens
Lippmann
Lois Lane (*Superman*)

Medill
Mergenthaler
Miss Thistlebottom (*Miss Thistlebottom's
    Hobgoblins,* Theodore M. Bernstein)

Nelly Bly (1st female reporter to cover hard news)
Non Sequitur

Oriana Fallaci

Pica (printing measure; also typeface)
Pulitzer
Pundit

Reston
Reuters
Roget
   (compiler of
   the Thesaurus)

Sanserif (typeface)
Scoop

Scripps-Howard
Spike
Syntax

Tabloid
Thesaurus

Verbatim
Virgule (slash mark)

Wally Ballou (reporter, Bob & Ray character)
Webster
Winchell
Woodstein (Bob Woodward & Carl Bernstein)

Eppie & Popo (Ann Landers & Dear Abby)
Funk & Wagnalls

Pairs:

Huntley & Brinkley
Merriam & Webster
Thorndike & Barnhart

Lawyers

Alibi
Alimony
Amicus Curiae (Lat., friend of the court)
A Priori (Lat., self-evident)
Archon (ancient Athenian chief of magistrates)
Astraea (Greek goddess of justice)

Bailiff
Barrister
Blackstone (English jurist)

Caducary (having to do with lapsed possessions)
Capias (writ ordering an arrest)
Cardozo (Supreme Court justice)
Caveat (legal notice not to act until notified;
    warning or caution)
Clarence Darrow
Cui Bono (Lat., Who benefits?)

Decus Tecum (Lat., with records)
De Jure (Lat., according to the law)

Docket
Double Jeopardy

Esquire

Fiat Justitia (Lat., Let justice be done)

Grotius (Dutch jurist, father of international law)

Habeas Corpus
Harlan
Hotchpot (common lot of properties divided in an
    estate)

Ipse Dixit (Lat., unproved assertion)
Ipso Facto (Lat., by that very fact)

Jacobellis (Supreme Court obscenity opinion)
J.D. (Lat., Juris Doctor, Doctor of Jurisprudence)
John Doe (hypothetical name)
John Law (personification of the police)

Judge Crater (judge who disappeared in August 1930)
Jurisprudence (philosophy of law)
Jus Divinum (Lat., divine law)
Justitia Omnibus (Lat., justice for all)

K.C. (King's Counsel, England)

Lex Non Scripta (Lat., common, or unwritten, law)
Lex Scripta (Lat., written or statutory law)
Lex Talionis (Lat., law of retaliation, "an eye for an eye")
Lord Chancellor (highest judicial officer in Britain)
Lord Chief Justice

Madam Justice
Mandamus (court command)
M.O. (Lat., modus operandi, method of operation)
Ms. Demeanor (misdemeanor, breaking the law, bad behavior)
Ms. Feasance (misfeasance, wrongful performance of a lawful act)
Ms. Prision (misprision, wrongful act, especially by a public official)

Mr. D.A. (Mr. District Attorney)

Nole Prosequi (intent to proceed no further)
Nolo Contendere (Lat., accepting conviction but not admitting guilt)
Non Sequitur (Lat., It doesn't follow)

Obiter Dictum (Lat., remark made in passing)
Old Bailey (London's chief criminal court)
Oliver Wendell Holmes

Palimony
Perjury
Perry Mason
Pettifogger (inferior lawyer)
Piso's Justice (verbally right but morally wrong)
Portia (lady barrister in *The Merchant of Venice*, Shakespeare)
Prima Facie (Lat., on the face of it)
Pro Bono Publico (Lat., for the public good)
Professor Kingsfield (*The Paper Chase*)

Q.B. (Queen's Bench, England)
Q.C. (Queen's Counsel, England)

Q.V. (Lat., as much as you like)

Rhadamanthus (son of Zeus, a judge of the dead)
Richard Roe (hypothetical name used on legal
    forms for 2nd person)

St. Yves (patron saint of lawyers)
Scofflaw (one who regularly flouts
    the law)
Snollygoster (illegitimate)

Themis (Greek goddess of justice
    & law)
Thurgood Marshall

Venue
Vinson
Voir Dire (Lat., direct questioning)

Pairs:

Assault & Battery
Martindale & Hubbell (directory of law firms)

Sui Generis & Sui Juris (unique & legally
    competent)

Literary Names

Adonaïs (poetical name given by Shelley to Keats in his elegy)

Anna Karenina (Tolstoy)

Artful Dodger (*Oliver Twist,* Dickens)

Aunt Pittypat (*Gone with the Wind,* Mitchell)

Auntie Mame (Patrick Dennis)

Avalon (paradise for medieval heroes)

Baron Munchausen (adventurous traveler)

Bartleby the Scrivener (Melville)

Becky Sharp (*Vanity Fair,* Thackeray)

Biddy (*Hard Times,* Dickens)

Billy Budd (Melville's innocent sailor)

Bloomsbury (literary and intellectual group in England after WWI)

Borogrove (nonsense word coined by Lewis Carroll)

Bounderby (*Hard Times*)

Bragi (Scandinavian god of poetry)

Buddenbrooks (Thomas Mann)

Bumble (*Oliver Twist*)

Bumper Morgan (*The Blue Knight,* Wambaugh)

Bunbury (urge to travel, *The Importance of Being Earnest,* Oscar Wilde)

Cacambo (*Candide,* Voltaire)

Calliope (Greek muse of epic poetry)

Calypso (sea nymph, *The Odyssey,* Homer)

Candide (Voltaire)

Captain Nemo (*20,000 Leagues Under the Sea,* Jules Verne)

Cardinal Richelieu (*The Three Musketeers,* Dumas)

Castalia (spring on Mount Parnassus, Greece; source of poetic inspiration)

Catullus (Alexander Hamilton's *nom de plume*)

Chloe (beloved maiden in pastoral literature)

Chuzzlewit (Dickens)

Circe (enchantress, *The Odyssey*)

Claggart (bully in *Billy Budd*)

Clare Quilty (*Lolita,* Nabokov)

Clemens (Mark Twain's real name)

Clerihew (humorous pseudo-biographical 4-line jingle)

Clio (Greek muse of history)

Colophon (ornamental inscription at beginning or end of a book)

Corleone (*The Godfather,* Puzo)

Count Vronsky (Anna Karenina's lover)

Cunegonde (Candide's lover)

David Copperfield (Dickens)

Decameron (Boccaccio)

Diggory (*Return of the Native,* Hardy)

Doctor Pangloss (philosopher in *Candide,* Voltaire)

Doctor Zhivago (Boris Pasternak)

Dodgson (Lewis Carroll's real name)

Dodsworth (Sinclair Lewis)

Dulcinea (love of Don Quixote)

Ebenezer Scrooge (*A Christmas Carol,* Dickens)

Elmer Gantry (Sinclair Lewis)

Elsinore (Hamlet's castle)

Epizeuxis (repetition of a word or phrase for emphasis)

Erato (Greek muse of love poetry)

Erewhon (Samuel Butler)

Esmeralda (Gypsy in *The Hunchback of Notre Dame,* Victor Hugo)

Euterpe (Greek muse of lyric poetry)

Evangeline (Longfellow)

Fabricius (wordy writer who made things unintelligible)

Faust

Fitz-Boodle (Thackeray)

Gareth (knight of the Round Table)

Garp (John Irving)

Gatsby (F. Scott Fitzgerald)

Gavroche (street arab, *Les Miserables,* Victor Hugo)

Gawain (knight of the Round Table)

Gigadibs (poet in *Bishop Blougram's Apology,* Browning)

Griselda (patient, romantic character, *The Decameron,* Boccaccio)

Grushenka (*The Brothers Karamazov,* Dostoyevsky)

Hafen Slawkenbergius (*Tristram Shandy,* Laurence Sterne)

Heathcliff (*Wuthering Heights,* Emily Brontë)

Hedda Gabler (Ibsen)

Helicon (poetic inspiration; flowing from green fountains)

Hester Prynne (*The Scarlet Letter,* Hawthorne)

Holden Caulfield (*The Catcher in the Rye,* J. D. Salinger)

Holly Golightly (*Breakfast at Tiffany's,* Capote)

Horatio Alger

Hudibras (satirical poem, Samuel Butler; means mock heroic)

Humbert Humbert (*Lolita*)

Iambic pentameter (poetic meter)

Ichabod Crane (*The Legend of Sleepy Hollow,* Washington Irving)

Invictus (poem by Henley; means unconquered)

Ishmael (*Moby Dick,* Melville)

Ithuriel (angel in Milton's *Paradise Lost;* means discovery of God)

Ivanhoe (Sir Walter Scott)

Jabberwocky (species of dragon, *Alice in Wonderland,* Lewis Carroll)

Jean Valjean (*Les Miserables*)

Jeeter (*Tobacco Road,* Caldwell)

Karamazov (Dostoyevsky)

Kipps (H. G. Wells)

Kizzy (*Roots,* Alex Haley)

Kunta Kinte (*Roots*)

Lady Chatterley (D. H. Lawrence)

Lady Marchmain (*Brideshead Revisited,* Evelyn Waugh)

Lady Teazle (*School for Scandal,* Sheridan)

Lady Windermere (Oscar Wilde)

Lapata (fictional land in *Gulliver's Travels,* Swift)

Launcelot (knight of the Round Table)

Lochinvar (Sir Walter Scott)

Lolita (Nabokov)

Lorbrulgrud (pride of the universe, *Gulliver's Travels*)

Lord Jim (Joseph Conrad)

Lord Marchmain (*Brideshead Revisited*)

Lucky Jim (Kingsley Amis)

Madame Bovary (Flaubert)
Madame Defarge (*A Tale of Two Cities,* Dickens)
Maecenas (ancient Roman patron of literature)
Mamamouchi (mock honor, spoofish title invented by Molière)
Manderley (mansion in *Rebecca,* Du Maurier)
Marjorie Morningstar (Herman Wouk)
Mimsy (Lewis Carroll nonsense word)
Miniver Cheevy (Edwin Arlington Robinson)
Miss Marker (Damon Runyon)
Miss Moneypenny (James Bond)
Mr. Bumble (*Oliver Twist*)
Mr. Goodbar (Judith Rossner)
Mr. Micawber (optimistic character, *David Copperfield*)
Mr. Quilp (*The Old Curiosity Shop,* Dickens)
Mr. Rosewater (Kurt Vonnegut)
Mr. Snagsby (*Bleak House,* Dickens)
Mrs. Dalloway (Virginia Woolf)
Mrs. Grundy (social arbiter, *Speed the Plough,* Thomas Morton)
Mrs. Jellyby (*Bleak House*)
Mrs. Malaprop (*The Rivals,* Sheridan)
Moby Dick (Melville)

Moll Flanders (Daniel Defoe)
Molly Bloom (*Ulysses,* James Joyce)
Monsieur Beaucaire (Booth Tarkington)

Nana (Zola)
Natty Bumppo (James Fenimore Cooper's old scout)
Nicholas Nickleby (Dickens)

Odysseus (*The Odyssey*)
Ozymandias (Shelley)

Palindrome (word or sentence reading the same backward as forward)
Parson Thwackum (*Tom Jones,* Fielding)
Passepartout (*Around the World in 80 Days,* Jules Verne)
Paul Bunyan (legendary hero of the American Northwest)
Peggotty (*David Copperfield*)
Pendennis (Thackeray)
Penrod (Booth Tarkington)
Percival (knight of the Round Table who found the Holy Grail)

Phileas Fogg (*Around the World in 80 Days,*
   Verne)
Phineas Finn (Trollope's Irishman)
Pip (*Great Expectations,* Dickens)
Polyhymnia (Greek muse of sacred poetry)
Poor Richard (Richard Saunders, Ben Franklin's
   pen name)
Porter (O. Henry's real name)
Portnoy (Philip Roth)
Presto (Jonathan Swift's name for himself)
Prufrock (T. S. Eliot)

Quasimodo (*The Hunchback of Notre Dame,*
   Victor Hugo)
Queequeg (*Moby Dick*)
Quentin Durward (Sir Walter Scott)

Raskolnikov (*Crime and Punishment,*
   Dostoyevsky)
Renfield (*Dracula,* Bram Stoker)
Romola (George Eliot)

Sadie Thompson (*Rain,* Somerset Maugham)
Salammbô (Flaubert)

Sartor Resartus (Thomas Carlyle)
Sebastian (*Brideshead Revisited*)
Shanachy (Irish traveling minstrel or storyteller)
Silas Marner (George Eliot)
Smiley (*The Spy Who Came In from the Cold,* Le
   Carré)
Starbuck (*Moby Dick*)
Stingo (*Sophie's Choice,* Styron)
Studs Lonigan (James T. Farrell)

Tara (*Gone with the Wind*)
Trimalchio (*Satyricon,* Petronius)
Tristero (*The Crying of Lot 49,* Thomas Pynchon)
Tristram Shandy (Laurence Sterne)

Ulysses (*The Odyssey*)
Uncle Vanya (Chekhov)
Uther Pendragon (knight of the Round Table)

Walter Mitty (James Thurber)

Yorick (jester's skull, *Hamlet*)
Yossarian (*Catch-22,* Joseph Heller)

Zossima (*The Brothers Karamazov*)   Zuleika Dobson (Max Beerbohm)

Pairs & Trios:

Athos, Porthos & Aramis (*The Three Musketeers,*
   Dumas)
Darby & Joan (loving couple from old English
   ballads)
Don Quixote & Sancho Panza (Cervantes)
Dr. Jekyll & Mr. Hyde (Stevenson)
Franny & Zooey (Salinger)
Hatfield & McCoy (feuding neighbors)
Lancelot & Guinevere
Little Eva & Topsy (*Uncle Tom's Cabin,* Stowe)
Mr. Rochester & Jane Eyre (Brontë)
Narcissus & Goldmund (Hermann Hesse)
Priscilla & John Alden
Scarlett & Rhett (*Gone with the Wind*)
Sherlock Holmes & Dr. Watson (A. Conan Doyle)
Vladimir & Estragon (*Waiting for Godot,* Beckett)

Medical

Aretaeos (father of medicine, title shared with Hippocrates)

Asklepios (Gr., medical practitioner; god of medicine and healing)

Ataraxia (medical term for peace of mind)

Babinski (test for infant normality)

Bilirubin (test for fertility)

Buscaglia (psychologist)

Caduceus (emblem of medicine)

Carl Jung

C.B. (Lat., Chirurgiae Baccalaureus, Bachelor of Surgery)

Chiron (Greek teacher famed for his medical skill)

Doc Holliday (*Gunsmoke*)

Dr. Ben Casey

Dr. Doolittle

Dr. Feelgood

Dr. Gillespie

Dr. Kildare

Dr. Livingstone

Dr. Quincy

Dr. Snapper Foster (*The Young & the Restless*)

Dr. Spock

Dr. Wasserman

Dr. Welby

EKG

Elizabeth Blackwell (1st woman doctor in U.S.)

Florence Nightingale

Galen (famous Greek physician)

Gurney (wheeled stretcher)

Hippocrates (Greek father of medicine, shared title with Aretaeos)

Hygeia (Greek goddess of health)

I.V.

Johns Hopkins

Kinsey

Locum Tenens (Lat., fill-in or substitute doctor)
Lydia Pinkham (nostrum for female ills)

Medicare
Medicaid

Nostrum
Nurse Ratched (*One Flew over the Cuckoo's Nest*)

ObGyn

Panacea (cure-all)
Paracelsus (Swiss physician who developed pharmacology)
Pavlov (Russian researcher and psychologist specializing in conditioning)
Placebo (control medicine, sugar pill)

Pritikin (nutritionist)

Q.E. (Lat., take daily, on prescriptions)
Q.S. (Lat., quantum sufficit, take as much as needed, on prescriptions)
Quassia (18th-century slave who discovered medicinal value of herbs)

Raphael (healing angel, the Bible)
Rorschach (test for emotional stability)

Salus (Roman goddess of health)
Sawbones (slang, surgeon)
Schweitzer (doctor who lived in Africa, treating natives)
Shamash (Babylonian god who protected against illness)
Sigmund Freud (father of psychoanalysis)
Simon-Binet (I.Q. test)
Stat (immediately)

Witch Hazel

Pairs:
Masters & Johnson

Military

Admiral
Alcibiades (ancient Athenian general)
Ammo
Andrea Doria (Genoese admiral)
Annapolis
Antietam (Civil War battle)
Appomattox (site where Civil War peace treaty was signed)
A-OK
Archibald (British slang, anti-aircraft gun; also Archie)
Askari (native soldier in colonial Africa)
As-U-Were
At Ease
Attila
AWOL (Absent Without Official Leave)

Ballista (ancient war machine that threw stones)
Bee-Bee (machine-gun bullet)
Beetle Bailey (comic strip)
Belisaurus (ancient Roman general)

Big Bertha (cannon)
Bivouac (camp outdoors)
Black Jack Pershing
Blunderbuss
Bogey (unidentified aircraft on radar screen)
Bomarc (ground-to-air antiaircraft missile)
Bosun
Bradley
Brigadier
Brown Bess (British Revolutionary War name for a flintlock musket)
Buccaneer
Busby (British guardsman's tall fur hat)

Captain Ahab (*Moby Dick*)
Captain Bligh (*Mutiny on the Bounty*)
Captain Queeg (*The Caine Mutiny*)
Casus Belli (Lat., cause for war)
Cataphract (ancient armor composed of metal scales)
Centurion (Roman soldier)

Cessna
Chamade (drum or trumpet signal for retreat or
    parley)
Chiang Kai-shek
Colonel Potter (*M*A*S*H*)
Commander
Commando
Commodore
CONAD (Continental Air Defense)
Concorde
Corsair
Custer

Dear John
Dixie (British slang for pot or pan)
Doughboy
Duke of Wellington

Eisenhower
Escadrille (unit in WWI of planes or warships)

Fantassin (Fr., infantryman)
Farragut
Fianna (Irish warriors)

Four-O (Navy slang, perfect)
Fourragère (braided cord indicating branch of the
    service)
Fusileer (British soldier with a musket)
Fuzzy-Wuzzy (Sudanese soldier)

Galloon (braid trim on uniforms)
General
Gettysburg
G.I. Bill

G.I. Joe
Golgotha (battlefield)
Grenadier (best soldier in the regiment)
Grumman
Gung Ho
Gyrene (Marine)

Hannibal (Roman general)
Holy Joe (chaplain)
Huff-Duff (high-frequency Air Force direction
    finder)

Jack Tar (British sailor)
JATO (jet-assisted takeoff)
Jimmy Doolittle
Joab (commander of King David's army)
Joe Gish (typical sailor)

Kamikaze
Khaki
Kilroy
Kitchener
K.P.

Lafayette
Lieutenant Pinkerton (*Madame Butterfly*)
Long Tom (large cannon)
Lord Nelson

MacArthur
Mach One (speed of sound in aeronautics)
Major Major (*Catch-22*, Joseph Heller)
Mameluke (Egyptian military rulers before the 16th
    century)
Merrimac
Mig Alley (area in Korean war where Communist
    jets began attacks on U.N. bombing missions)
MIRV
Mr. Ducrot (West Point term of derogation toward
    plebes)
Mister Roberts
Montezuma
Montgomery
M.P.
Mufti (civilian clothes)

Napoleon

NASA (National Aeronautics and Space Administration)
NATO (North Atlantic Treaty Organization)
Nimitz
Noncom (Noncommissioned Officer, or NCO)
NORAD (North American Air Defense Command)

O.D. (olive drab)
Old Salt
Old Soldier
ONI (Office of Naval Intelligence)

Patton
Pentagon
Pequod (ship in *Moby Dick*)
Plebe (lowest-class member at Military or Naval Academy)
Poggie (Army recruit)
Pom-Pom (antiaircraft gun)
Private Benjamin
Private Hargrove
P.T.-109 (Kennedy's patrol boat, Petey)

QF (quick-firing)
QMC (Quartermaster Corps)

Rackensacker (slang, state militiaman)
Rajput (member of the Hindu military ruling class)
Repple-Depple (slang, replacement depot, where soldiers await reassignment)
Re-Up (reenlist)
Reveille
Rickover
Robert E. Lee
Rotacy (R.O.T.C.)
R and R (rest and recreation)

Sad Sack
Sam Browne (officer's belt)
Sarge
Scuttlebutt (rumor)
Semper Fidelis (Marine Corps motto: always faithful)
Semper Paratus (Coast Guard motto: always prepared)
Sepoy (formerly, an Indian who was a soldier in the British Army)

Sergeant York
SHAEF (Supreme Headquarters Allied
   Expeditionary Forces)
Shavetail (newly commissioned 2nd lieutenant)
Silver Star (medal awarded for gallantry in action)
Skipper
Skirmish
SNAFU (Situation Normal—All Fouled Up)
Snowdrop (slang, member of the Military Police)
Soogie Moogie (Navy slang, scrubbing the deck)
S.O.P. (Standard Operating Procedure)
Spam
Stonewall Jackson

Ten Hut (attention)

Horatio & Hornblower
Roger & Wilco

Tipperary
Tommy Atkins (British soldier)
Torpedo

U. S. Grant

Vicksburg (Civil War battle)
Vinegar Joe (Gen. Joseph Stilwell)
Von Clausewitz (Prussian military strategist)

Wellington
Winchester

Yardbird (rookie)
Yeoman

Pairs:

Rookie & Tenderfoot
Trafalgar & Waterloo (Napoleon's defeats)
Willie & Joe (Bill Mauldin WWII soldiers)

Mixed Breed

Anthology

Bouillabaisse (Fr., fish chowder)
Burgoo (Brunswick stew)

Casserole
Cassoulet (meat-and-bean casserole)
Charretse (Ger., pot-luck supper, scraped together)
Chop Suey
Chowder
Cioppino (seafood soup)

Dinty Moore

Eintopf (Austro-Ger., bean-and-meat casserole)
Etcetera

Farrago (confused state)
Filius Nullius (Lat., son of nobody, illegitimate)
Foo Chow (blend of teas)
Fricassee

Gallimaufrey (hash, a jumble)
Goulash
Gumbo

Heinz '57
Hodgepodge, Hotch-Potch

Jambalaya
Jumble

Kedgeree (casserole)

Lorelei

Macedoine (Fr., mixed fruits)
Medley
Melange
Minestrone
Mishling (Ger., hybrid, crossbreed)
Mishmash
Miss Celany (Miscellany)
Mosaic
Mulligan Stew

Olla Podrida (Span., hodgepodge)

Omnium-Gatherum (Lat., miscellaneous collection or mixture)

Pasticcio (medley)
Pastiche (Fr., mixed)
Patchwork
Pot-au-Feu (chicken casserole)
Potpourri

Ragout (Fr., stew)

Salmagundi (casserole)
Salpicon (casserole)

Zakuski (Russian hors d'oeuvre)

Pairs:

Flotsam & Jetsam (debris after an ocean storm)

Patches & Scraps

Movies

Andy Hardy
Annie Hall
Antonioni

Bacall
Bakshi
Barbarella
Batjac (John Wayne's production company)
Beckett
Bela Lugosi
Belmondo
Bertolucci
Best Boy (technical term for movie grip)
Billy Dee
Billy Wilder, Gene Wilder
Bluto (*Animal House*)
Bo Derek
Bogdanovich
Bogey
Brando
Brewster McCloud

Brigitte Bardot
Buford T. Justice
Buñuel
Butterfly McQueen

Cagney
Carmen Miranda
Carradine
Cassavetes
Cat Ballou
Cato (Inspector Clouseau's butler, *The Pink Panther*)
Cecil B. De Mille
Cesar Romero
Chaplin
Chauncey Gardiner (*Being There*)
Chewbacca (*Star Wars*)
Cinema
Citizen Kane
Clara Bow
Cloris Leachman

Cooga Mooga (Pat Boone's production company)
Coppola
Costa-Gavras

Dalton Trumbo
Darth Vader (*Star Wars*)
De Niro
Diamond Lil
Dietrich
Disney
Dobie Gillis
Doctor Strangelove
Douglas Fairbanks
Duddy Kravitz
Durante
Dustin Hoffman

Eisenstein
Elsa (*Born Free*)
Elvira Madigan
Erich von Stroheim
Errol Flynn
E.T.

Fatty Arbuckle
Fay Wray
Fellini
Finzi Contini

Gable
Garbo
Gay Purree
Gazzara
Georgy Girl
Gidget
Gigi
Godzilla
Goldie Hawn
Goldwyn
Griffith
Gypsy Rose Lee

Han Solo (*Star Wars*)
Harlow
Harry O
Hermione Gingold
Hieronymus Merkin
Hitchcock

Indiana Jones (*Raiders of the Lost Ark*)
Inspector Clouseau (*The Pink Panther*)
Ish Kabibble (actor; also slang, "I'm not worrying")

James Dean
Jaws

Karloff
Kazan
Kitty Foyle
Klute
Kovacs
Kubrick

Lando Clarissian (*Star Wars*)
L. B. Mayer
Lina Wertmuller
Linda Lovelace
Lollobrigida
Lon Chaney
Lubitsch
Luke Skywalker (*Star Wars*)

Mae West

Malpeso (Clint Eastwood's production company)
Marcello Mastroianni
Mazursky
Melina Mercouri
Merle Oberon
Mia Farrow
Mickey Rooney
Minnelli
Mr. Lucky
Mrs. Miniver
Mrs. Robinson
Modesty Blaise
Moms Mabley
Monty Woolley

Natacha Rambova (Valentino's love, a set
    designer)
Nickelodeon
Nimoy
Norma Jean (Marilyn Monroe's real name)

007
Obi-Won Kenobi (*Star Wars*)
Olivier

Omar Sharif
Oscar
Oz

Pacino
Peckinpah
Pennebaker (Brando's production company)
Pepe Le Moko ("Come wiz me to ze Casbah")
Pier Angeli
Pink Panther
Polanski
Pola Negri
Popi
Preminger
Princess Leia Organa (*Star Wars*)
Putney Swope

Quackenbush (Woody Allen's production
   company)

Raimu
Ramon Novarro
Raul Julia
Robards

Rocky
Rosebud (*Citizen Kane*)
Rossano Brazzi
Rossellini
Rouben Mamoulian

Sal Mineo
Scatman Cruthers
Sean Connery
Selznick
Shirley Temple
Slappy White
Slim Pickens
Sophia Loren
Stanwyck
Stella Dallas
Stepin Fetchit

Tab Hunter
Tallulah
Tara
Tartoonie (planet in *Star Wars*)
Telly Savalas
Terry-Thomas

Thalberg
Theda Bara
Tootsie
Travolta
Tron
Truffaut
Tyrone Power

Ustinov

Valentino
Visconti

Waldo Pepper

WAMPAS (pre-Oscar award to most promising
   new star)
W. C. Fields
Wildwood (Robert Redford's production company)
Woody Allen

Yoda (*Star Wars*)

Zanuck
ZaSu Pitts
Zoetrope (Coppola's production company)
Zohra Lampert
Zorba
Zorro
Zsa Zsa

Pairs, Trios & Quartets:

Abbott & Costello
Bonnie & Clyde
Buster & Keaton
Cheech & Chong
Harold & Maude
Harpo, Chico, Groucho & Zeppo Marx
Harry & Tonto

Jabba & Jedi (*Star Wars*)
Laurel & Hardy
Minnie & Moskowitz
Olsen & Johnson (Ole & Chic)
Redford & Newman
Smokey & Bandit
Tracy & Hepburn

Music

A Capella (singing without instrumental accompaniment)

Aïda (opera by Verdi)

Alan-a-Dale (minstrel follower of Robin Hood)

Allargando (Ital., slower and louder)

Allegretto (Ital., a little briskly)

Allegro (Ital., lively)

Almaviva (*The Barber of Seville,* Rossini)

Amadeus

Amati (maker of stringed instruments, 1596–1684)

Amoroso (Ital., with tenderness)

Amphion (son of Zeus, skilled on the lyre)

Andante (Ital., moderately slow)

Andantino (Ital., slightly faster)

Appassionato (Ital., impassioned)

Arco (Ital., music direction to resume using bows)

Aretha Franklin

Arietta (Ital., short song)

Arioso (Ital., songlike)

Arpeggio (notes of a chord in rapid succession)

ASCAP (musicians' union)

Babaloo

Balalaika

Bamboula (African dance with drums)

Bandore (old-time guitarlike instrument)

Banjo

Bartok

Basilio (*The Barber of Seville*)

Bebop

Beethoven

Belafonte

Bel Canto

Benedictus (short hymn)

Berlioz

Bix Beiderbecke

Bizet

Blossom Dearie

Blushington (*Utopia, Ltd.,* Gilbert & Sullivan)

Bo Diddley

Bolero

Bongo
Boogie-Woogie
Bouzouki (Greek banjolike instrument)
Boz Skaggs
Brio (Ital., vivacity)
Brubeck
Bubbles (Beverly Sills' nickname)
Buddy Holly

Cab Calloway
Caccini (composer)
Calando (Ital., gradually diminishing in tone and pace)
Calliope (instrument with steam whistles)
Callithumpian (noisy concert with beating of tin pans and catcalls)
Calypso (improvised song)
Cantabank (strolling singer)
Cantata (choral work)
Cantino (treble string of stringed instrument)
Capotasto (device on fretted instrument to raise the pitch)
Capriccio (Ital., lively, whimsical)

Capriccioso (Ital., free, fantastic style)
Captain Macheath (*The Threepenny Opera,* Kurt Weill)
Carmen (opera by Bizet)
Caruso
Catalani (composer)
Cavatina (short, simple song or melody)
Cenerentola (opera, Cinderella, Rossini)
Chaliapin (opera singer)
Chalumeau (clarinet's lowest register)
Chanterelle (E string of the violin)
Chanteuse (Fr., female singer)
Charivari (mock serenade of noise; callithumpian)
Charlie Mingus
Cherubini (composer)
Cherubino (page in *The Marriage of Figaro,* Mozart)
Chevalier
Chubby Checker
Cio-Cio-San (*Madame Butterfly,* Puccini)
Ciribiribin (Harry James's theme song)
Cithara (ancient lyrelike instrument)
Clarabella (organ stop that produces sweet tones)
Clarino (early type of trumpet with high register)

Con Affetto (Ital., tenderly, with feeling)
Conway Twitty
Count Danilo (*The Merry Widow,* Franz Lehar)
Crosby

Da Capo (Ital., from the beginning)
Dandini (*La Cenerentola*)
Demisemiquaver (32nd note)
Didgeridoo (Australian natives' instrument that
    makes a wailing sound)
Dithyramb (Greek choral song in honor of
    Dionysus)
Diva (female opera singer)
D.J.
Dolby (sound system)
Dolly Parton
Don Basilio (music master in *The Marriage of
    Figaro*)
Don Giovanni (opera by Mozart)
Donizetti (composer)
Don Magnifico (*La Cenerentola*)
Don Pasquale (opera by Donizetti)
Dooley Wilson
Dr. Bartolo (*The Barber of Seville*)

Duke Ellington
Dvořák
Dylan

Eartha Kitt
Elton John
Elvis Presley
Engelbert Humperdinck
Eroica
Escamillo (*Carmen*)
Euterpe (Greek muse of music and lyric poetry)

Fabian
Fa-La-La
Fats Domino
Fenice (opera house, Venice)
Fiddle
Fidelio (Beethoven)
Fitzbattleaxe (*Utopia, Ltd.*)
Fleetwood Mac
Fortissimo (Ital., very loud)
Frasquita (Gypsy in *Carmen*)

Galli-Curci

Gamba (viola and cello combination)
Gershwin
Gianni Schicchi (opera by Puccini)
Glinka (composer)
Glissando (violin technique, sliding over the
    strings)
Grammy (record-industry award)
Guarnerius (violin maker)
Gustav Mahler (composer)

Harmony
Haydn (composer, father of the symphony)
Heifetz (violinist)
Hi-Fi
Hindemith (composer)
Honky-Tonk
Hootenanny
Hurdy-Gurdy (hand organ)

Impresario
Iolanthe (Gilbert & Sullivan)
Itsy-Bitsy Teeny-Weeny Yellow Polka-Dot Bikini (hit
    song of 1960s)

Johnny Cash
Jolson
Jomelli (composer)
Joplin (composer; also singer Janis Joplin)
Josephine Baker
Jubal (inventor of stringed and wood instruments,
    Genesis)
Juilliard

Katisha (*The Mikado,* Gilbert & Sullivan)
Katya Kabanova (opera by Janaček)
Kazoo
Kenny Rogers
Khachaturian (composer)
Kirsten Flagstad (opera singer)
Klingsor (magician in *Parsifal,* Wagner)
Ko-Ko (*The Mikado,* Gilbert & Sullivan)
Kostelanetz (conductor)
Koussevitzky (conductor)
Kris Kristofferson

Lady Day (Billie Holiday's nickname)
Lalo (composer)

La Scala (opera house, Milan)
Leadbelly (Huddie Ledbetter, folk singer)
Led Zeppelin
Leontyne Price
Liberace
Libretto
Lillie Langtry
Little Richard
Lohengrin (opera by Wagner)
Lorelei (legendary German singing siren)
Lotte Lenya
Lucia di Lammermoor (opera by Donizetti)
Lucy Lockit (*The Threepenny Opera*)
Lynnard Skynnard

Madrigal (love poem set to music for several voices)
Maestro, Maestra (conductor)
Magnificat (Lat., utterance of praise)
Mahalia Jackson
Makeba (singer)
Mancini
Manilow
Manon Lescaut (opera by Puccini)

Marcellina (duenna in *The Marriage of Figaro*)
Marimba
Mario Lanza
Mascagni (composer)
Meat Loaf (singer)
Meistersinger (opera by Wagner)
Melba (opera singer)
Melodeon (small organ)
Melodia (organ)
Melody
Melomania (mania for music)
Mendelssohn
Meno Mosso (Ital., not so fast)
Menotti
Merman
Mick Jagger
Mikado (Gilbert & Sullivan)
Mimi (*La Bohème*, Puccini)
Minnie Pearl
Minnie the Moocher
Mirabella (*The Gypsy Baron*, Johann Strauss)
Mistinguette (singer)
Molly Malone
Montemezzi (composer)

Motown
Moussorgsky (composer)
Mozart
Musetta (*La Boheme*)
Muzak

Nabucco (opera by Verdi)
Nadia Boulanger (music teacher)
Nanki-Poo (*The Mikado*)
Naughty Marietta (operetta by Victor Herbert)

Obbligato (accompaniment to a solo)
Odetta
Offenbach (composer)
Oom-Pa-Pa
Ormandy (conductor)
Orpheus (played the lyre so sweetly animals and
    rocks followed him)
Ostinato (Ital., constantly repeated melody)
Otis Redding

Paderewski (composer)
Paganini (violinist and composer)
Pagliacci (opera by Leoncavallo)

Palestrina (composer)
Pamina (*The Magic Flute,* Mozart)
Papageno (bird-catcher in *The Magic Flute*)
Parsifal (opera by Wagner)
Partita (series of dance tunes for several
    instruments)
Patachou
Pavarotti
P.D.Q. Bach
Peep-Bo (*The Mikado*)
Percy Grainger (composer)
Piccolo (instrument; also Ital., small)
Pierre Boulez (conductor)
Pink Floyd
Pitti-Sing (*The Mikado*)
Pizzicato (violin technique, plucking the strings)
Placido Domingo

Poco a Poco (Ital., little by little)
Polly Peachum (*The Threepenny Opera*)
Polonaise (Chopin)
Poo-Bah (*The Mikado*)
Prima Donna
Prince Igor (suite by Borodin)
Prokofiev (composer)
Puccini (composer)
Purfling (inlaid border on violin)

Quodlibet (whimsical combination of familiar melodies)

R&B (rhythm and blues)
R&R (rock and roll)
Rachmaninoff
Rallentando (Ital., slowing down)
Ravi Shankar
Renata Tebaldi (opera singer)
Reno Sweeney
Rhapsody (resembling an improvisation)
Riff (improvisation in jazz)
Rigoletto (opera by Verdi)
Ringo Starr

Ritornello (instrumental part for solo or choral voice)
Rockabilly
Rondeau (Fr. tune that keeps coming around)
Rosalia (melodic phrase repeated several times, consecutively higher)
Rosa Ponselle
Rosenkavalier (opera by Richard Strauss)
Rossini
Rubato (Ital., give-and-take in tempo)
Ruddigore (Gilbert & Sullivan)

Saint-Saëns (composer)
Salieri (composer)
Salome (opera by Richard Strauss)
Salsa (Latin American beat)
Saltato (allowing the bow to spring back)
Samisen (Japanese guitarlike instrument)
Sarinda (Indian stringed instrument)
Sassy Sarah Vaughan
Scarlatti (composer)
Scarpia (police chief in *Tosca,* Puccini)
Scat (fast singing of gibberish words)
Scherzando (Ital., playful)

Scherzo
Schubert (composer)
Schumann (composer)
Scoobie Doobie Doo
Sedaka
Segovia (guitarist)
Seiji Ozawa (conductor)
Sibelius (composer)
Simon Boccanegra (opera by Verdi)
Sinatra
Skimmington (English burlesque serenade to a
   henpecked husband)
Sonata
Sophie Tucker
Sordino (Ital., soft pedal)
Sousa
Spiccato (short, springing movements of the bow)
Springsteen
Steinway (piano)
Stevie Wonder
Stokowski (conductor)
Stradivarius (violin maker)
Stravinsky (composer)
Streisand

Subito (Ital., suddenly)
Sukey Tawdry (*The Threepenny Opera*)

Tambourine
Tamino (Egyptian prince in *The Magic Flute*)
Tannhäuser (opera by Wagner)
Ta-Ra-Ra-Boom-De-Ay
Tchaikovsky (composer)
Terpander (father of Greek music)
Thelonius Monk
Timpani
Tin Pan Alley
Tira Tutti (Ital., pull out all the stops, in organ
   music)
Toccata (composition for the piano or organ to
   show off the performer's technique)
Tomtom (drum)
Toplady (English clergyman who wrote "Rock of
   Ages")
Tosca (opera by Puccini)
Toscanini (conductor)
Traviata (opera by Verdi)
Tremolando (Ital., with a wavering tone)

Truffaldino (*The Love for Three Oranges,*
   Prokofiev)
Turandot (opera by Puccini)
Tutti (Ital., full orchestra)

Ukulele

Van Cliburn
Verdi (composer)
Violetta (*La Traviata*)
Vivace (Ital., lively)
Vivaldi (composer)

Wagner (composer)

Waylon Jennings
Woodstock
Woody Guthrie
Wotan (Wagnerian hero)

Yehudi Menuhin
Yma Sumac
Yoko Ono
Yum-Yum (*Mikado*)

Zarzuela (Spanish operetta)
Za Za (opera by Leoncavallo)
Zerlina (country girl in *Don Giovanni*)
Zinka Milanov (opera singer)
Zubin Mehta

Pairs & Trios:

Boris & Godunov
Frankie & Johnny
Gilbert & Sullivan
Lerner & Loewe
Major & Minor
Peaches & Herb
Pelléas & Mélisande (Debussy)

Ping, Pang & Pong (*Turandot,* Puccini)
Porgy & Bess (Gershwin)
Rimsky & Korsakov
Rodgers & Hammerstein
Siegfried & Brünnhilde
Simon & Garfunkel
Tony Orlando & Dawn
Tristan & Isolde (Wagner)

Mythology & the Ancient Classics

Achilles (Greek warrior at Troy)
Adonis (handsome youth, loved by Aphrodite)
Aeneas (Trojan hero, Aphrodite's son)
Agamemnon (king who led the Greeks in the Trojan War)
Agrippina (Emperor Nero's mother)
Ajax (hero at Troy)
Amphitryon (legendary Greek lavish host, prince of Thebes)
Andromeda (daughter of Oedipus and Jocasta)
Anubis (Egyptian conductor of the dead in the nether world)
Ashtoreth (Phoenician goddess of love)
Atalanta (Greek maiden famed for her speed in running)
Atlas (carrier of the sky)
Augustus (Roman emperor)
Aurelia (Julius Caesar's mother)

Baldur (Scandinavian god of light)

Bellerophon (Greek hero who killed the Chimera)
Ben Hur
Brahma (Hindu creator)
Brigit (Celtic goddess of hearth, fire & poetry)
Busiris (mythical king of Egypt)

Caesar (Roman emperor)
Caligula (Roman emperor and despot)
Callisto (nymph)

Cassandra (daughter of King Priam, given the gift of prophecy, but no one believed her)

Cassiopeia (mother of Andromeda)
Charon (boatman who ferried the dead to Hades)
Chrysippus (stolen baby who caused the Oedipus
    tragedy)
Cicero (Roman orator)
Claudius (Roman emperor)
Clytemnestra (Agamemnon's wife)
Cratos (personification of force)
Croesus (very rich king)

Daedalus (father of Icarus)
Damocles (courtier in Syracusan king's court)
Demosthenes (Athenian orator)
Deucalion (son of Prometheus, ancestor of the
    human race)
Diogenes (Greek philosopher who wandered,
    seeking an honest man)
Dodona (oracle of ancient Greece)
Donar (German god of thunder)

Echo (nymph who pined away with love)
Electra (Agamemnon's daughter)
Endymion (beautiful youth loved by the moon
    goddess)

Epigoni (sons of heroes in the war against Thebes)
Epimetheus (brother of Prometheus, husband of
    Pandora)

Fafnir (Scandinavian legendary dragon guarding
    the Nibelung's treasure)
Favonius (the west wind)

Ganymede (cup bearer to the gods)
Gilgamesh (legendary Babylonian king)

Hadrian (Roman emperor)
Harmonia (daughter of Aphrodite)
Heliogabalus (Roman emperor)
Horatius (Roman hero)

Iphigenia (Agamemnon's daughter)

Jason (leader of the Argonauts)
Jocasta (Oedipus' mother)
Justinian (Roman emperor)

Loki (Scandinavian god of mischief)

Melampus (Greek seer who could talk with animals)
Mercedonius (extra month in Roman calendar)
Messalina (Emperor Claudius' wife)
Morpheus (Greek god of sleep and dreams)

Nero (Roman emperor)
Nibelung (German mythical dwarf)
Niobe (Queen of Thebes)

Odin (chief Scandinavian god)
Oedipus (Greek king who unwittingly killed his father and married his mother)
Olympia (Mt. Olympus, home of the gods)
Orestes (Agamemnon's son)

Pandora ("all-gifted," keeper of everything to ruin mankind)
Pericles (Athenian statesman and military commander)
Persephone (daughter of Zeus; symbolic of the 4 seasons)
Phaedra (wife of Theseus, king of Athens)

Phidippus (descendant of Hercules)
Plutus (Greek god of riches)
Prometheus (descendant of the gods, a Titan)
Psyche (symbolic of the human soul or spirit)

Sabrina (nymph)
Saturnalia (ancient Roman revels)
Semiramis (ancient Assyrian princess said to have founded Babylon)
Spartacus (Roman warrior)
Strabo (Greek geographer; means squint-eyed)

Tantalus (son of Zeus who betrayed the gods' secrets)
Theseus (Greek hero who killed the Minotaur)
Thetis (mother of Achilles)
Thor (Scandinavian god of thunder)
Tiberius (Roman emperor)
Titus (Roman emperor)

Vespasian (Roman emperor)

Xanthippe (Socrates' wife; a scolding wife)

Pairs:

Anshar & Kishar (Babylonian gods of heaven & earth)

Damon & Pythias (symbols of devoted friendship)

Daphnis & Chloe (lovers)

Heloise & Abelard (lovers)

Hero & Leander (lovers)

Jason & Medea

Orpheus & Eurydice

Priam & Hecuba

Pygmalion & Galatea

Remus & Romulus (sons of Mars, founders of Rome)

Scylla & Charybdis (rock and whirlpool)

Troilus & Cressida (lovers)

Greek and Roman Gods and Goddesses

Greek

Zeus (king)   Hera (queen)

Phoebus; also Helios or Hyperion (sun)

Ares (war)

Hermes (messenger)

Poseidon (ocean)

Hephaestus (fire and forge)

Demeter (harvest)

Artemis (moon and hunting)

Athena (wisdom)

Aphrodite (love and beauty)

Hestia (home)

Roman

Jupiter or Jove (king)   Juno (queen)

Apollo

Mars or Quirinus

Mercury

Neptune

Vulcan

Ceres

Diana or Dido (Phoenician name)

Minerva

Venus

Vesta

Dionysus (wine)   Ariadne (wife)   Bacchus
Eros (love)   Cupid
Pluto (the infernal regions)   Persephone (wife)   Pluto   Proserpine (wife)
Cronus (time)   Saturn or Cleodorus

The 9 Greek Muses:

Calliope (epic poetry)   Polyhymnia (sacred poetry)
Clio (history)   Terpsichore (dance)
Erato (love poetry)   Thalia (comedy)
Euterpe (lyric poetry)   Urania (astronomy)
Melpomene (tragedy)

The 3 Fates: Clotho, Lachesis & Atropo
The 3 Furies: Magaera, Alecto & Tisiphone
   (ti-SIF-o-nee)
The 3 Graces: Agalia, Thalia & Euphrosyne
   (yew-FRO-se-nee)
The most ancient god: Chaos (personifies
   nothingness before the universe)

Personality

Ambidexter
Ambush
Andrasteia (Greek goddess of inevitable fate, later
  Nemesis)

Ballyhoo
Bandit
Banshee
Bedlam
Blinky
Bodacious (slang, bold and audacious; reckless)
Bohunk (slang, rough fellow)
Bonkers (Brit. slang, crazy)
Boomerang
Brouhaha (fuss)
Bruiser
Bumpkin
Buttinsky (interrupter, interloper)

Calamity Jane
Caper

Carouser
Casanova
Charisma
Chaser
Conundrum (puzzle)
Copasetic (wonderful)
Cuddles
Curiosity
Curmudgeon

Daedal (DEE-dal, ingenious)
Dandy
Dapper Dan
Dapperling (little dapper fellow)
Dexter (of or on the right-hand side)
Discordia (Roman goddess of dissension)
Don Juan
Donnybrook (brawl)
Draggletail (obsolete, wanton)
Dreampuss

Elan (charm)
Enigma

Fanfaron (fanfare)
Feisty
Felice, Felicity
Fiasco
Fiddle-Faddle
Fidget
Folly
Foofaraw (fuss
    over trivialities)
Forty Winks
Fracas
Furor

Gadabout
Gallivanter
Gigolo
Girandole (spinning firework)
Glammapuss
Globetrotter
Gusto
Gypsy

Heliophilous (sun-loving)
Hobo
Hogen-Mogen (high in might; strong)
Hooligan
Hoopla
Hubris (pride; arrogance)

Inglenook (the corner by the fire)
Isadorable
Ivan the Terrible (Tsar of Russia, 1530—1584)

Jester
Jim Dandy

Know-It-All

Larrikin (Australian slang, hoodlum)
Lazy Bones
Lazy Susan
Lickerish (fond of choice food)
Lickety-Split
Lightning
Lollygag
Lothario

Macho Man, Macho Mouser
Maelstrom (confusion; whirlpool)
Me-Too
Meowzer
Mischief
Mordacious (given to biting)
Morpheus (Greek god of sleep and dreams)
Moxie
Mr. Clean
Ms. Behavin'
Mumpsimus (obstinately holding on)
Myrmidon (obedient follower; loyal)

Nibbles
Nimblefoot
Nimrod (hunter)
Nomad
Nook-Shotten (running into corners)
Nosy Parker
Nuzzles

Panache (flair)
Paragon (model of excellence)
Peccadillo

Peeping Tom
Perdu (hidden away, out of sight)
Perky
Persnickety (fussy)
Philander (fickle)
Pizzazz
Pococurante (indifferent)
Pouncer
Prowler
Puzzle

Q.T. (quiet)
Quandary (perplexed)
Quicksilver
Quietus (state of inactivity)
Quotidian (reappearing daily)

Ragamuffin
Rambler
Ramstam (impetuous, reckless)
Rantipole (boisterous and wild)
Rapscallion
Rascal
Razzmatazz

Rebus (puzzle)
Richochet
Riffraff
Rocket
Rowdy
Rumbustious (unruly, boisterous)
Rumpus

Saccharine
Sassy
Scairdy Cat
Scarper (Brit. slang, leave in a hurry)
Siesta
Skedaddle
Skulduggery (rascally)
Sloomy (obsolete, sleepy)
Sly Boots
Sly Puss
Smarty Pants
Sneaky Pete
Snuggles
Spelunker (cave explorer)
Spizzerinktum (slang, vigor)
Sprinter

Spunky
Stormy
Sugar Baby
Sugar Daddy
Sugarino
Sunshine
Swellelegant
Swifty

Tagalong
Theodorable
Tinkerpaws
Tintinnabulary Tabby (bell-ringer)
Tirrivee (angry outburst)
T.N.T.
Tourbillon (spiral firework)
Tranquility
Triboulet (court fool of Louis XII)
Trouble
Tuffy
Twinkle, Twinkletoes

Valentine
Vamp

Vesuvius
Virago (warriorlike woman)

Wanchancy (dangerous; uncanny)
Wanderlust
Whisper
Whizbang

Wikiwiki (weekee-weekee, Hawaiian, quickly)
Willy Nilly
Winky

Zesty
Zippity Doodah
Zonkers

Pairs:

Bouncer & Bounder
Dilly & Dally
Dither & Tizzy
Helter & Skelter
Hither & Thither
Hotsy & Totsy
Hunky & Dory
Jeepers & Creepers
Pip & Squeak
Rack & Ruin
Razzle & Dazzle

Scamper & Scatter
Shilly & Shally
Skidoo & Skedaddle
Skimble & Skamble (rambling & silly)
Snazzy & Spiffy
Sugar & Spice
Teeter & Totter
Topsy & Turvy
Twixie & Tweenie
Vim & Vigor
Whatchamacallit & Thingamajig
Zig & Zag

Physical Characteristics

Algernon (Fr., bewhiskered)
Anurous (tail-less)

Bandy (bowlegged)
Bangles
Big Ben
Bijou (jewel; fine and small thing; trinket)
Brighteyes
Buskin (knee-high boot)
Buttons

Daddy Longlegs
Dinky (little)
Dundreary (side-
  whiskers)

Ember

Fiona (Gaelic, fair)

Glimmer

Half-Pint
Hop-o'-My-Thumb

John L. Lewis (former head of coal miners who
  had very bushy eyebrows)

Lilliputian (tiny people in *Gulliver's Travels*, Swift)
Lionelle (lionlike)
Llewellyn (Celtic, lionlike)
Lollapalooza (beauty)

Meowderpuff
Michu (smallest star in the circus, 33 inches tall)
Minikin (diminutive creature)
Minimus (very small creature)
Mittens
Modicum (small quantity)
Mr. Whiskers
Mustachio
Mutchkin (Scottish unit of liquid measure less than
  1 pint)

Nimbus (halo)

Pantaloon
Patches
Pebble
Pinky
Polydactyl (having extra toes)
Pygmy

Slippers
Small Fry
Smidgen
Sneakers
Sockdollager (remarkably large or strong; the
   ultimate)

Soupçon (very small amount)
Spats
Splendiferous

Tassels
Thimble
Tidbit
Tom Thumb
Trinket

Velvet

Wallydrag (Scottish, youngest and smallest in the
   litter)
Whiskers

Pairs:

David & Goliath
Hurly & Burly

Itsy & Bitsy
   Maxi & Mini

Giants & Amazons

Alifanfaron (*Don Quixote,* Cervantes)

Behemoth (huge biblical animal)
Blunderbore ("Jack the Giant Killer")
Bremusa (Amazon)
Brobdingnag (country of giants, *Gulliver's Travels,* Swift)

Colossus
Corflambo ("Jack the Giant Killer")
Cormoran ("Jack the Giant Killer")

Enceladus (100-armed giant)

Ferracute (giant with the strength of 40 men)

Galligantus ("Jack the Giant Killer")
Gerryoneo (*Faerie Queen,* Spenser)
Goliath
Grangousier (father of Gargantua)
Grantorto (giant typifying rebellion, *The Faerie Queen*)

Hercules
Hippolyta (queen of the Amazons; daughter of Mars)

Leviathan

Megalonyx (Lat., giant claw)

Orgoglio (*The Faerie Queen*)

Polydorus (*The Iliad,* Homer)
Porphyrion

Quinbus Flestrin ("man mountain," *Gulliver's Travels*)

Radigund (queen of the Amazons, *The Faerie Queen*)

Skrymir (Scandinavian giant)

Thalestris (queen of the Amazons; bold, heroic female)

Ymir (Norse giant of ice and fire who became the universe)

Gargantua & Pantagruel

Pairs:

Gog & Magog (British giants)

Gray Cats

Ashfurrd
Aurora (Lat., dawn)

Chiaroscuro (kee-ah-ro-SKOO-ro, light and dark)
Chloris (Gr., pale)
Cinerous (ashy hue)

Dorian Gray
Dusty

Ghost
Grisaille (gree-ZYE)

Gurei (Jap., gray)

Nezumi (Jap., mouse)

Phantom
Plumbeous (leaden)
Pogonip (icy mountain fog)
Pussywillow

Shadow
Smoky

Umbrageous (shaded; also easily insulted)

Varicolored/Yellow Cats

Aurelia (Lat., golden)
Aurum (Lat., gold)

Blondie
Butterscotch

Catechin (yellow dye)
Clinquant (glittering with gold)
Curry

Dijon (mustard)

Filemot (yellowish brown)
Flavia, Flavian (Lat., yellow)
Flavicant (yellowish)

Marmalade
Meerschaum
Melina (Lat., yellow)

Patches
Poupon (mustard)

Quercetin (yellow pigment)
Quercitron (yellow dye)

Saffron
Sherry
Smudges

Xanthe (Gr., golden)
Xanthin (yellow)
Xanthos (Gr., yellow)

Black Cats

Albertite (jet-black mineral)
Anthracite (coal)
Apollo Creed (*Rocky*)
Atro Ceruleous (blackish-blue)
Aubergine (Fr., eggplant)

Bituminous (coal)
Blacula

Charcoal
Cherni (Rus., black)
Cimmerian (very dark)
Cinder; Cinderella

Dee (Welsh, black)
Demitasse (black coffee)
Duff (Celtic, dark, male)

Ebony
Eclipse
Emperor Jones (Eugene O'Neill)

Fusain (charcoal for drawing)

Golliwog (turn-of-the-century black doll)

Hottentot

Inky

Karamazov (Rus., black)
Kuro (Jap., black)

Li (Chinese, black)
Licorice

Mavi (Armenian lucky blue-black stone)
Melantha (Gr., dark flower)
Midnight

Obsidian (black volcanic glass)
Onyx

Satchmo
Sooty

White Cats

Alabaster
Alba (Lat., white)

Bianca (Ital., white)
Blanca (Span., white)
Blanche (Fr., white)
Blizzard
Buttermilk
Byell (Rus., white)

Candida (Lat., pure white)
Chantilly (lace)

Fionnula (Gaelic, white-shouldered)
Frosty

Glacier

Malako (Rus., milk)

Marshmallow
Milky Way
Misty

Nevada (Span., snow-white)
Nivea (Lat., snow-white)

Phoebe Snow

Shiro (Jap., white)
Snowball
Snowdrop
Snowflake

Tundra

Vanilla

Yuki (Jap., snow)

Brown/Reddish/Orange Cats

Alpenglow (rosy hue seen near mountain peaks)

Barbarossa (Ital., red-beard)
Bricktop
Brindle
Bruno (Ital., brown)
Buffy

Café au Lait (Fr., light coffee)
Cappuccino
Carnelian
Carrot-Top
Cayenne
    (pepper)
Cheroot
    (cigar)
Chocolate
Cinnabar
    (red mineral)
Cinnamon
    (Canella, Ital.)

Cocoa
Cocoa-Puff

Ginger

Java

Kahawa (Swahili, coffee)
Kahlua
Ketchup
Kid Chocolate

Kona (coffee)
Kumquat

Maduro (dark cigar)
Melachrino (cigarette)
Mocha
Mojave (mo-HAH-vay, desert)
Mosca (Ital., coffee bean)

Nutmeg

Orange Julius

Palisander (rosewood)
Panatella (slim cigar)
Paprika

Penny
Pepper
Persimmon

Red Buttons
Red Ryder
Rubicund (rosy)
Rufus (reddish)
Ruskin (red-haired)
Russell (red-haired)
Rusty

Sahara
Sanka
Sepia
Sienna

Black-&-White Cats

Bausond (white patch on forehead or white stripe
   down face)

Domino

Harlequin

Panda

Tuxedo

Color of Eyes

Amber

Celadon (pale green)
Cerulean (sky blue)
Chatoyant (sha-twah-YAHN, changeable color or
    luster)

Emerald

Iola (Gr., violet cloud)
Iona (Gr., violet-colored stone)

Jade
Jasper

Koki (Jap., glitter)

Malachite

Mazarine (deep, rich blue)
Mica (silvery, shiny rock)

Okin (Jap., gold)
Opan

Peridot (yellowish-green gem)

Sapphire
Sapphirine (pale blue or green)

Topaz
Turquoise

Verdigris (light green that copper turns when it
    oxidizes)

Wedgwood (blue)

Politics

Abscam
Adlai Stevenson
Alf Landon
Also Ran

Ben Franklin
Bismarck
Bolivar (bo-LEE-var)
Bolshevik (Russian radical, pre-Revolution, 1917)
Boodle (slang, graft)
Boondoggle (useless work)
Boss Tweed
Buckley

Calvin Coolidge
Catherine the Great (Russian empress)
Chiang Kai-shek
Chou En-lai
Churchill
Clemenceau
Colonel Blimp (ultraconservative Englishman)

Cromwell

Daniel Webster
D.C.
De Gaulle
Demosthenes (great Athenian statesman)
Dewey
Disraeli
Dolley Madison
Doonesbury

Fianna Fail (Irish separatist political party)
Filibuster
Fiorello
Franklin Delano
Frederick the Great

Gerrymander
G.O.P.

Haile Selassie

Herbert Hoover
Hubert Humphrey

Jackson
Jefferson Davis

Kissinger
Kosciusko

Lacey Davenport (*Doonesbury*)

L.B.J.
Lincoln
Lloyd George
Locofoco (supporter of Andrew Jackson's
    presidential campaign, 1833)
Lulu (payment in lieu of expenses)

Machiavelli
Mao Tse-tung
Mark Russell (political satirist)
McKinley
Menshevik (Russian liberal, pre-Revolution, 1917)
Millard Fillmore

Mugwump (independent Republican, 1884)

Potemkin (Russian adviser to Catherine the Great)
Perle Mesta (hostess during Truman
    Administration)

Robespierre (political leader of the French
    Revolution)

Scalawag (Southern Democrat)
Senator
Stonewall Jackson

Talleyrand
Tammany
Throttlebottom (Vice President in *Of Thee I Sing*)
T.R. (Teddy Roosevelt)
Truman

Van Buren
Veep
Veto

Washington

Watergate
Wendell Willkie

Woodrow Wilson

Grits & Fritz (Carter & Mondale)
Rough & Ready (nickname for Zachary Taylor)

Pairs:

Sacco & Vanzetti
Tippecanoe & Tyler Too

Scientists & Mathematicians

Archimedes (Greek mathematician and inventor)
ASME (American Society of Mechanical Engineers)

Boffin (British slang, theoretical scientist or engineer)
Brinell (Swedish engineer who devised a metal-hardness standard measurement)

Calculus
Coriolis (French mathematician)

Darwin

Edison
Enrico Fermi
Euclid (ancient Greek mathematician)
Ex Pede Herculem (Lat., from this sample, judge the whole)

Galileo (mathematician and astronomer)
Goddard (father of rocketry)
Googol (the number 1 followed by 100 zeroes)

Isaac Newton (mathematician and astronomer)

Logarithm

Madame Curie
Mantissa (decimal part of a logarithm)
Marconi
Mochis (inventor of weights and measures)
Monad (indivisible unit)

Nonillion (the number 1 followed by 30 zeroes)

Octillion (the number 1 followed by 27 zeroes)

Philomath (lover of learning, especially math or
 science)
Pie R Square
Pythagoras

Quantal (1 or 2 alternatives)

Quantum (quantity)
Quark (smallest sub-atom)
Quasar (energy)

Slide Rule

Wankel

Pairs:

Geometry & Trigonometry
Hypotenuse & Isosceles

Radar & Sonar
Wilbur & Orville (Wright)

Sports & Games

Abner Doubleday (reputed inventor of baseball)
Ace
Agon (Greek athletic contest)
A. J. Foyt
Ambsace (smallest point in dice throw)
Ante Up
Arcaro
Aunt Sally (British game played at fairs)

Babe Didrikson
Babe Ruth
Baccarat
Backgammon
Badminton
Barney Oldfield
Big Mac (McEnroe)
Billie Jean
Black Jack
Blooper
Bobble
Bocci

Bogey
Bricole (pool shot; indirect or unexpected action)
Broadway Joe (Namath)
Bucky Dent
Bunter

Cahill (artificial fly for fishing)
Caissa (humorously, goddess of chess)
Campanella
Canasta
Capablanca (international grand chess master)
Casey Stengel
Casino
Catfish Hunter
Checkmate
Chemin de Fer
Chips
Colonel Bogey (imaginary golf player with
    assigned score to beat)
Cosell
Cribbage

Croupier (gambling-table attendant)

Decathlon
Dempsey
DiMaggio
Dipsy-Doodle (curve ball in baseball)
Discobolus (ancient Greek discus thrower)
Divot
Dizzy Dean
Dodger
Domino
Doubleton (having only 2 cards in a suit in a
    bridge hand)
Dundee (boxing promoter)
Durocher

Easley Blackwood (bridge expert)
Equilabrist (acrobat)
Evel Knievel
Exacta (horse parlay)

Fantan
Faro
Finesse (bridge move)

Flambeur (Fr., gambler)
Foozle (bungle a golf stroke)
Fulham (dice loaded at the corners)
Fungo (practice fly ball in baseball)

Gambit
Gentleman Jim (Corbett)
Givoco Piano (slow chess game)
Gipper
Goren
Grand Prix
Gridiron

Half Nelson
Hat Trick
Henley (boat-race site in England)
Hobie Cat (sailboat)
Homer (home run)
Hoyle (book of game rules)

Jai Alai
Jersey Joe (Walcott)
Jim Thorpe
John L. Sullivan

Joker
Junior

Kalouchi (card game)
Kareem Abdul-Jabbar
Karpov (Russian chess champ)
Kayo (K.O., knockout)
Kibitz (Yiddish, offer unsolicited advice)
Knute Rockne
Koufax

Lacrosse
Lotto

Mah Jong
Maris
Martingale (doubling the stakes at cards)
Marquess of Queensberry (formulated rules for
    boxing)
Mashie (no. 5 iron in golf)
Mathias
Mazzilli
Meadowlark Lemon
Mickey Mantle

Minnesota Fats (pool champ)
Mosconi (pool champ)
Muhammad Ali
Mulligan (permissible 2nd drive off the 1st tee
    without a penalty)

Nadia Comaneci
Nastase
Navratilova
Niblick (golf club, especially to get out of sand
    traps)
Nicklaus
Nimzo Indian (chess defense)
Northpaw (right-handed player)

O. J. Simpson

Palaestra (Greek gymnasium)
Palooka
Pancho Gonzalez
Parchesi
Parimutuel
Pee Wee Reese
Pelé

Pétanque (pay-TANK, French lawn ball game)
Philidor (international grand chess master)
Pimlico
Pinochle
Pistol Pete
Polydamas (famed Greek athlete of immense size
    and strength)

Quinella (picking 1st and 2nd winners at the dog
    races)
QB (chess, queen's bishop)

Rappel (descending a steep slope on a rope when
    mountain climbing)
Reggie
Rhubarb (fight at a ball game)
Riffle (a hard swing with the bat; also to shuffle
    cards)
Rizzuto
Robinson
Rookie
Rosey Grier
Roulette
Royal Flush

Rugby (or Rugger)

Satchel Paige
Schneider
Scrabble
Scrimmage
Scroogle (screwball pitch)
Shoeless Joe
Shortstop
Slalom
Slapshot
Slugger
Solitaire
Southpaw
Spadelle (queen of clubs)
Steinbrenner
Stymie (golf ball blocking the hole)
Sugar Ray

Tartakover (international grand chess master)
T.D. (touchdown)
Thurmond
T.K.O. (technical knockout)
Trevino

Ty Cobb

Valenzuela
Vigorish (percentage paid to the banker in cards)

Wallenda (circus acrobat family)
Weeb Ewbank (former N.Y. Jets coach)
White Sox
Willie Joe (Namath)
Willie Mays
Wimbledon
Wotjek Fibak (VOY-check FEE-back)

Yarborough (bridge hand with nothing higher than
   a 9)
Yastrzemski
Yogi

Pairs & Trios:

Acey & Deucey
Hart, Schaffner & Marx (3 jacks in poker)
Tinker, Evers & Chance (baseball infield oldies)
Trump & Reneg

Theater

Ad Lib
Admirable Crichton (J. M. Barrie's infinitely
   resourceful butler)
Ado Annie (*Oklahoma*)
Albee
Aldonza (*Man of La Mancha*)
Applause
Ariel (*The Tempest,* Shakespeare)

Banquo (*Macbeth,* Shakespeare)
Barrymore
Beaumont
Belasco
Blanche Dubois (*A Streetcar Named Desire,*
   Tennessee Williams)
Boffo (a hit)
Boffola (belly laugh)
Bravo
Brigadoon
Broadway Baby
Brutus (*Julius Caesar,* Shakespeare)

Burleycue (Burlesque)

Caliban (*The Tempest*)
Camelot (Rodgers and Hammerstein)
Candida (George Bernard Shaw)
Catastasis (3rd part of ancient dramas, before the
   catastrophe)
Cordelia (*King Lear,* Shakespeare)
Coriolanus (Shakespeare)
Cymbeline (Shakespeare)
Cyrano de Bergerac (Rostand)

Damrosch
Desdemona (*Othello,* Shakespeare)
Dolly Levi (*Hello, Dolly!*)
Ducat (slang, ticket)
Dulcamara (1st play by W.S. Gilbert, without
   Sullivan)
Duncan (*Macbeth*)

Eliza Doolittle (*My Fair Lady*)

Elsinore (Hamlet's castle)
Emcee (M.C., master of ceremonies)
Encore

Falstaff (*The Merry Wives of Windsor,*
   Shakespeare)
Fantoccino (puppet)
Finian (*Finian's Rainbow*)

Garrick
Gielgud
Glocca Morra (fictional country, *Finian's
   Rainbow*)

Henry Higgins (*My Fair Lady*)
Horatio (*Hamlet,* Shakespeare)

Iago (*Othello*)

Kathacali (Indian pantomime)
Kudos (critical acclaim)

Laertes (*Hamlet*)
Leblang (slang, to sell theater tickets at cut rates)

Liliom (Ferenc Molnar)
Little Mary Sunshine
Lysander (*A Midsummer Night's Dream,*
   Shakespeare)
Lysistrata (Aristophanes' feminist anti-war heroine)

Macbeth
Macduff (*Macbeth*)
Major Barbara (Shaw)
Marquee
Melpomene (Greek muse of tragedy)
Mercutio (*Romeo and Juliet,*
   Shakespeare)
Minsky
Mr. Wonderful
Mrs. Lovett (*Sweeney Todd*)
Molière

Nathan Detroit (*Guys and Dolls*)
Nellie Forbush (*South Pacific*)
Nicely Nicely (*Guys and Dolls*)

Oberon (*A Midsummer Night's Dream*)
Odeon (theater or music hall)
Odeum (Greek and Roman theater)
Old Vic (London theater)
Oliver
Orlando (*As You Like It,* Shakespeare)
Ovation

Perdita (*The Winter's Tale,* Shakespeare)
Petruchio (*Romeo and Juliet*)
Pierrot
Pippin
Pirandello
Polonius (*Hamlet*)
Prospero (*The Tempest*)
Puck
Punchinello (clownlike character in Italian puppet shows)

Quinapalus (*Twelfth Night,* Shakespeare)

Ralph Rackstraw (*H.M.S. Pinafore,* Gilbert & Sullivan)
Ruby Dee

Saroyan
Scapino
Scaramouche
Sganarelle (comic character in Molière comedies)
Sky Masterson (*Guys and Dolls*)
Stanislavsky (creator of Method acting)
Sweeney Todd

Tamora (*Titus Andronicus,* Shakespeare)
Tartuffe (Molière)
Terence Rattigan
Thalia (Greek muse of comedy)
Thespis (father of Greek tragedy)
Thomashefsky
Thornton Wilder
Timon (disliker of mankind, *Timon of Athens,* Shakespeare)
Titus Andronicus (Shakespeare)
Tony (theater award)
Trinculo (*The Tempest*)

Volpone (Ben Jonson)

Willy Loman (*Death of a Salesman,* Arthur Miller)

Yorick (*Hamlet*)

Zero Mostel
Ziegfeld

Pairs & Trios:

Antony & Cleopatra
Beatrice & Benedict
Bijou, Roxy & Apollo
Caesar & Cleopatra
Hamlet & Ophelia
Lunt & Fontanne
Montague & Capulet (*Romeo & Juliet*)

Punch & Judy
Romeow & Juliet
Rosencrantz & Guildenstern (*Hamlet*)
Ruby Dee & Ossie Davis
Summer & Smoke (Tennessee Williams)
Tandy & Cronyn
Tevye & Golde (*Fiddler on the Roof*)

Titles

Ambassador

Babu (Hindu title meaning sir)
Baron Munchausen
Bishop
Bonnie Prince Charlie
Bretwalda (Lord of the Britons, title given to early
   Saxon kings)

Catherine the Great
Chairman Meow
Contessa
Count Danilo (*The Merry Widow*)
Count Vronsky (*Anna Karenina*)
Countess

Duchess
Duke

Empress

Frederick the Great

Grand Panjandrum (mock title for imaginary
   personage of importance)

H.I.H. (His/Her Imperial Highness)
H.I.M. (His/Her Imperial Majesty)
Honcho

Imperator (supreme ruler in Roman times)

Lord Chancellor (highest judicial officer in Britain)
Lord Fauntleroy
Lord High Admiral
Lord Snowden

Magnifico (Venetian nobleman)
Major Domo (in charge of the household)
Marchioness
M'Lady
M'Lord

Mohammed

Pasha (former Turkish title of rank)
Pendragon (title of ancient British chiefs)
Pharaoh (Egyptian king)
Prince Igor (opera by Borodin)
Prince Orlofsky (*Die Fledermaus,* Johann Strauss)
Princess
Professor

Queenie

Regina (Lat., queen)
Rex (Lat., king)
R.W. (Right Worthy or Right Worshipful)

Sahib
Sovereign
Sultan
Suzerain (feudal lord)
Swami

Tsarina
Tunku (Malayan title of prince)

Your Majesty

Pairs:

Prince Albert & Queen Victoria
Prince Charles & Lady Di

Queen Elizabeth & Prince Philip

TV & Radio

AFTRA (American Federation of Television and
  Radio Artists)
Annette Funicello
Arbitron (television rating system)
Archie Bunker

Baba Wawa (*Saturday Night Live*)
Baby Snooks
Banacek
Baretta
Barnaby Jones
Barney Miller
Beaver Cleaver
Benson
Bosley (*My Three Angels*)

Captain Furillo (*Hill Street Blues*)
Captain Merril Stubing (*The Love Boat*)
Chano (*Barney Miller*)
Charo
Cher

Chevy Chase
Clio (advertising award)
Columbo

Donahue
Duffy (*Duffy's Tavern*)
Durward Kirby

Eliot Ness
Emily Latella (*Saturday Night Live*)
Emmy (television award)

Flip Wilson
Fonzie
Frank Perdue
Freeman Gosden (Amos, of *Amos 'n Andy*)

Gilligan
Gomer Pyle
Gonzo (*Trapper John*)
Guido Sarducci (*Saturday Night Live*)

Hawkeye (*M*A*S*H*)
Helen Trent
Herve Villechaize (*Fantasy Island*)
Honeycutt (*M*A*S*H*)
Howdy Doody

Illya Kuryakin (*The Man from U.N.C.L.E.*)
Imogene Coca
Ironside

Joe Piscipo (*Saturday Night Live*)
John Boy (*The Waltons*)
Johnny Fever (*WKRP in Cincinnati*)

Kaz
Kojak
Kotter

Lamont Cranston (*The Shadow*)
Latka (*Taxi*)
Lisa Loopner (*Saturday Night Live*)
Lou Grant
Love Sidney
Luba Potamkin

Madam Foxy Humdinger (*Days of Our Lives*)
Magnum P.I.
Mannix
Ma Perkins
Margo Lane (The Shadow's girlfriend)
Mary Hartman, Mary Hartman
Merton Harmerdoit (professional fool, Bob and Ray character)
McCloud
McGarrett (*Hawaii Five-O*)
Minicam
Mr. Spock (*Star Trek*)
Mr. Sulu (*Star Trek*)
Mrs. Calabash (Jimmy Durante signature, "Good night, Mrs. Calabash, wherever you are.")

NAB (National Association of Broadcasters)
Napoleon Solo (*The Man from U.N.C.L.E.*)
Nielsen (television rating system)
Nipsy Russel

Orson Bean
Our Gal Sunday

Phoebe Tyler (*All My Children*)
Ponch (*CHiPS*)

Radar (*M*A*S*H*)
Regis Philbin
Renko (*Hill Street Blues*)
Roddenberry (creator of *Star Trek*)
Rodney Dangerfield
Rosanne Rosannadanna (*Saturday Night Live*)
Rourke (*Fantasy Island*)
Rulla Lenska

St. Elsewhere
Sergeant Esterhaus (*Hill Street Blues*)
Sitcom
Stella Dallas
Steverino
Swoosie Kurtz

Amos & Andy
Bates & Coffey (*Hill Street Blues*)

Tattoo (*Fantasy Island*)
Trapper John
Trekky

Uncle Miltie

Video

Pairs:

Cagney & Lacey
Charlie McCarthy & Mortimer Snerd

Cramden & Norton (*The Jackie Gleason Show*)
Curley, Moe & Larry (The 3 Stooges)
Desi & Lucy
Donny & Marie Osmond
Edgar Bergen & Charlie McCarthy
Felix & Oscar (*The Odd Couple*)
Fibber McGee & Molly
Fred & Ethel (*I Love Lucy*)
Fred & Wilma (*The Flintstones*)

Friday & Smith (*Dragnet*)
George (Burns) & Gracie (Allen)
Latka & Simca (*Taxi*)
Laverne & Shirley
Mork & Mindy
Ozzie & Harriet
Starsky & Hutch
Tate & Campbell (*Soap*)
Wally & Beaver (*Leave It to Beaver*)

Writers, Poets & Philosophers

Aeschylus (father of Greek tragedy)
Aesop
Aldous Huxley
Alice B. Toklas
Anaïs Nin
Anaximander (Greek philosopher, 500 B.C.)
Aristophanes (father of comedy)
Aristotle
Aurore Dupin (George Sand's real name)

Baedeker
Balzac
Baudelaire
Boccaccio
Boswell
Boz (Charles Dickens' *nom de plume*)
Bradbury
Brontë
Bruce Catton
Byron

Camus
Capote
Castaneda
Catullus (Alexander Hamilton's *nom de plume*)
Cervantes
Chaucer
Cheever
Chekhov
Chrysippus
Cicero
Coleridge
Conan Doyle

Damon Runyon
Dante
Dashiell Hammett
Dickens
Dostoyevsky

E. B. White
e. e. cummings

Emerson
Emily Dickinson
Erasmus
Euripides

Faulkner
Feiffer
Flaubert

Gallico
Gertrude Stein
Gogol

Hardy
Hemingway
Henry Miller
Herodotus
H. G. Wells
Hipponax (Greek father of parody)
Homer
Horace

Ibsen
Ionesco

Kafka
Kerouac
Kahlil Gibran
Kierkegaard

Langston Hughes
Longfellow
Lord Byron
Lucretius

Malagrowther (Sir Walter Scott's *nom de plume*)
Malraux
Marcel Proust
Maxim Gorky
Maya Angelou
Mencken

Nabokov

Nietzsche

O'Casey
Ogden Nash
O. Henry
Orwell
Oscar Wilde
Osceola (one of Isak Dinesen's *noms de plume*)
Ovid

Paddy Chayefsky
Pascal
Pellegrina (one of Isak Dinesen's *noms de plume*)
Pirandello
Plato
Plimpton
Pliny
Plutarch
Pushkin
Puzo

Quercus (Christopher Morley's *nom de plume*)

Rabelais

Racine
Rimbaud
Rudyard Kipling

Saint-Exupéry
Saki
Sandburg
Sappho
Sardou
Schopenhauer
Shakespeare
Socrates
Solzhenitsyn
Sophocles
Spenser
Spinoza
Steinbeck
Stendhal
Strindberg
Studs Terkel

Tacitus
Tarkington
Tennyson

Terpander
Thackeray
Thoreau
Thucydides
Thurber
Tolstoy
Trelawney (Shelley's companion)
Trollope
T. S. Eliot
Turgenev

Unamuno

Victor Hugo
Virgil
Voltaire
Vonnegut

Whitman
Wordsworth

Xenophon

Zola